Dedicate

I want to dedicate this book to all the great leaders who have changed my vision and perspective on Leadership & Project Management. They inspired me with their characteristics, ethics, and the work they deliver to better the community. I want to thank them for not only shaping my mind; they have restructured and shaped my character as a leader & as a Leader. I learned many new aspects of Project Management during my collaboration with the leaders, which has actually drive me crazy to put across my thoughts and insights. I want to name those leaders in this book who has shaped my mind and character as a Project Manager. They all are truly inspiring, and they always offer a lot to society. Those leaders are **Satish Krishnappa, Sunil Arunodaya, Marc Vanschoenwinkel, Gaurav Dhooper, Kartikeyan Ramamurthy, Harriet Green, Gaurang Vora, Mani Selvan Nyana Jothi, Sridhar K, Leonardo Reyes Torres, Americo Pinto, Priya Patra, and Varun Anand.**

All these leaders influenced me so much to write articles. I never thought that I would be written 45+ articles in just seven months. It's not just writing articles; they also expand my Project Management knowledge during these months. It is an honor to work with all these great leaders and learning from them is more than equivalent to achieve any level of certifications. So, thanks for inspiring me and helping me to transform. I owe for what I am right now.

Envisioning PMO & Project Management through a Juggler's Eye: Part-1

A BOOK OF DIFFERENT VISION & PERCEPTION

ABHISHEK MISHRA

Copyright © Abhishek Mishra
All Rights Reserved.

This book has been published with all efforts taken to make the material error-free. The author does not assume and with this disclaim any liability to any party for any loss, damage, or disruption caused by errors or omissions, whether such errors or omissions result from negligence, accident, or any other cause.

Every effort is made to avoid any mistake or omission. The publication sold on the condition and understanding that neither the Author nor Publisher would be liable in any manner to any person because of any mistake or omission in this publication. Any action is taken or omitted to made or advice rendered or accepted based on this work. This book or any portion of this book may not reproduce or be used in any manner whatsoever without the author or the Publisher's prior permission.

Disclaimer: This is a work of fiction. Names, characters, businesses, places, events, locales, and incidents are either the products of the author's imagination or used in a fictitious manner. Any resemblance to actual persons, living or dead, or actual events is purely coincidental.

Contents

- **Dedicate**
- **Introduction**
- **Chapter-1:** How to Set up a PMO
- **Chapter-2:** How to create a PMO Framework
- **Chapter-3:** Key PMO Roles and Responsibilities
- **Chapter-4:** What is Project Governance and The Process to Create an Effective Governance Framework
- **Chapter-5:** Process of developing a PMO strategic Plan
- **Chapter-6:** Tips for Managing the Project Budget
- **Chapter-7:** Aligning Project Management with Business Strategy
- **Chapter-8:** Project Managers - Are they, Warriors or Bookkeepers
- **Chapter-9:** What is EPMO? and How do we differentiate both the groups and manage both the groups seamlessly
- **Chapter-10:** The Secrets of Successful EPMOs
- **Chapter-11:** Common Project Management Mistakes and how to avoid such mistakes
- **Chapter-12:** Project Managers have the skills to become CEOs, but why they don't
- **Chapter-13:** Spotify Scaling Agile Model
- **Chapter-14:** Digital Transformation
- **Chapter-15:** Blending Project Management with Quantum Physics
- **Chapter-16:** Revolutionize Project Management with Artificial Intelligence, Machine Learning, and Predictive Analytics
- **Chapter-17:** Remote Project Management
- **Chapter-18:** How to make Remote Project Management Work
- **Chapter-19:** The Hybrid Methodology the Freedom to Project Management approach
- **Chapter-20:** Hybrid Project Management: The Blended Project Management Methodology

- **Chapter-21:** What does P Stand for in PMO
- **Chapter-22:** How to Cook up a Meal out of Project Management
- **Chapter-23:** The Identity Crisis of a PMO in the age of Digital and Agile Trends
- **Chapter-24:** How did I transform myself into a better Project Manager
- **Disclaimer**
- **About the Author**

I have one of my quotes that remains very close to me "Don't limit your challenges; in fact, keep challenging all your limits, then the real miracle will happen, and the true character will be unveiled" - Abhishek Mishra. The quality of a successful and great leader is selfless thinking. A person who feels insecure and thinks of themselves can be a good manager but not a leader. So, thanks to all of you for letting me know the actual definition of the word called "selfless." Thank you for teaching, guiding, and directing me in every phase of my life. I dedicate my professional career to all of you.

*Lastly, I would like to especially thank my wife, **Sailaja Mishra**, who has been a tremendous support to me and encouraged me to write books.*

Introduction

Envisioning PMO & Project Management through a Juggler's Eye does not mean that I have created some complex framework or Methodology. It is all about my view of PMO and Project Management. I have tried explaining the vital aspects of Project Management and PMO through my articles; all my articles can provide insight into how someone can start looking at Project Management and PMO as a character, not just as a skill.

This book is a structural compilation of my articles. I will represent my selected 24 articles out of my 46 articles in the first part and then the remaining in the second part.

Project managers can become CEO's, and they have all the skills and competencies to make it to the CEO's level. I have assessed some of the justifications why, currently, few PMs get there and what they need to do to make it to the top of the career ladder. Please find more details in Chapter#12.

Whenever I asked my friends or colleagues what "P" stands for in the PMO, I always got a standard answer that it is "Project," "Program," and "Portfolio," but in my opinion, it is "Power," "Pioneer" and "Potential." Would you like to know how? I have mentioned it in detail in Chapter#21.

How, with a little replication, you could make yourself a better Project Manager; even though you do not have a mentor, you do not prefer to read long and complicated books, you can still be a better Project Manager and a better leader. I followed some of the simple steps to transform myself. Sounds exciting right, for more details, please refer to chapter#24

The name "Quantum Physics" sounds very interesting, and considering the principles of Quantum Physics, it is worth evaluating its potential in relation to Project Management, risk management, and prioritization. Quantum Physics has its root in the management of uncertainty. The uncertainty is the key factor behind the deviation that can occur during project execution. It can also add a lot more value to Risk Management and Prioritization. Do you want to find out how? Then please refer to chapter#15 for more details.

I am presenting Twenty-four such articles that can provide you a completely different view and knowledge on PMO and Project Management. I hope you will like all those 24 chapters, which I earlier published as an article on multiple platforms.

Chapter-1

How to Set up PMO

Introduction

I have been doing lots of research on "how do we go about getting an effective PMO started?". The large organizations with many projects and programs have learned that having a PMO will bring value to the table and an organization. These large organizations have been willing to stay focused, and many of them have already established an effective PMO group, and organizationally accepted project processes. Several kinds of research further say; the value proposition has become murkier for mid-sized and smaller organizations. The willingness to stay focused on implementing project processes wavers with fluctuations in business conditions. To ensure all the organizations that already have a mature PMO group and processes and to the ones who are considering establishing a PMO group and the associated processes can always refer to the basics to get it right. It is significant to understand the PMO architecture, to have an effective PMO set up.

Project Management Office Architecture

The groups that had established PMO's agree with the functional description above for their PMO's. The groups with no PMO's are interested in getting started and what pitfalls were encountered by those who had been through the implementation of PMO and

Project management processes. I tried to create an architectural diagram for the PMO setup, given below.

Here is the PMO architecture diagram

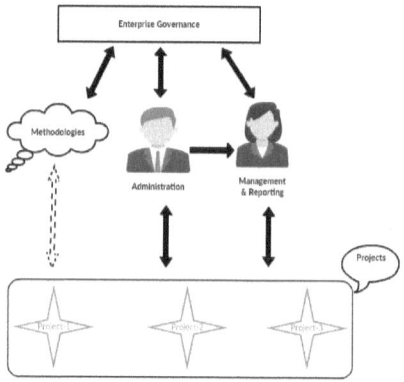

The above mentioned architectural diagram follows through a PMO roadmap, and the architectural diagram and roadmap always compliment each other. The group consensus on what tasks to focus on in starting a PMO function in a mid-sized or smaller organization will revolve around the tasks mentioned in the PMO roadmap.

Project Management Office Roadmap

Creating a roadmap that is adaptable and flexible according to your respective organizational needs would require you to spend a modest amount of time and require an equal amount of effort to brainstorm the activities in detail to come up with a conclusion. Here is a roadmap, which is more on a general front, and this can be modified according to the organizational need or requirement.

Definition of Scope – Senior Management Perspective
- *Any existing discussion*
- *Any recognized pain points*
- *Identify the strategic objective*

Identify target business areas
- *Pain Points*
- *Existing projects*
- *Future/ Planned projects*
- *Project Sizes*

Impact of Organization acceptance/change
- *Realistic assessment*
- *Understand/determine where potential gains can be made*

Identify "As Is" Processes and tools
- *Project scheduling tools*
- *Reporting tools*

- *Cost budgeting tools in place*

Identify potential champions
- *Conduct meetings/presentations to communicate the results of the above.*

Taking the time to do an analysis outlined above will allow an organization to thoroughly understand its need and its capacity to implement and absorb a more formal PMO and project management process approach.

PMO's Nuts & Bolts

To establish and work with PMO's it required specific characteristics that can be relatable during the implementation phase of PMO and project processes. Those characteristics are defined in three sections: methodologies, Administration, and Management & reporting. Let's understand in detail.

Methodologies
- Need the ability to support multiple methodologies.
- Required to have minimum documentations
- Creating templates for ease of acceptance.

Administration
- Detail data is required
- Time-tracking - Any time-tracking tool like Pro, Ultipro, OpenAir, Spring ahead, clarity, or maybe anyone suitable to the respective organization.
- Schedules - MS Project, Primavera, Smartsheet, HP-

PPM, etc.

- Issues with redundant time-tracking
- Integration with corporate financial/ planning system
- Paying attention to schedule and cost

Management & Reporting
- Coordination with corporate goals and objectives
- Definitions of KPIs
- Tools to distill details into KPI's - QuickBase, Project Servers, Service now, Jira, Salesforce cloud commerce
- Pay attention to schedule and cost
- Run projects based on the defined processes, guidelines, and best practices.
- Measure Projects outcome and ensures the project follows the processes and best practices.

PMO Process Flows

Now I would like to highlight few processes, flows that are based on PMO processes; those are the followings:

- The project proposal process
- The project planning process
- The project execution process
- The project closeout Process

Here I have created the detailed flow of all the PMO processes mentioned earlier and their outputs.

The Project Proposal Process
Outputs:

- Project Submission form
- Project Scoring tool
- Risk assessment model

Here I have presented the overall flow and architecture of the IT PMO project proposal process.

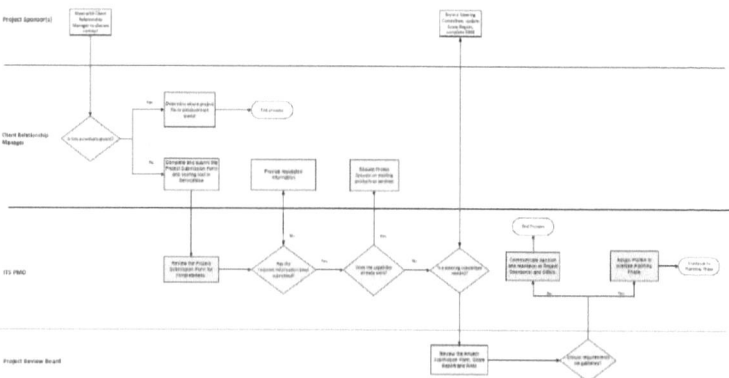

The Project Planning Process
Outputs:

- Project Statement
- Process Diagrams
- Requirements Document
- Cost-Benefits analysis
- Work Breakdown Structure
- Resource Plan

Here I am adding the snapshot of the IT PMO project planning process's overall flow and architecture.

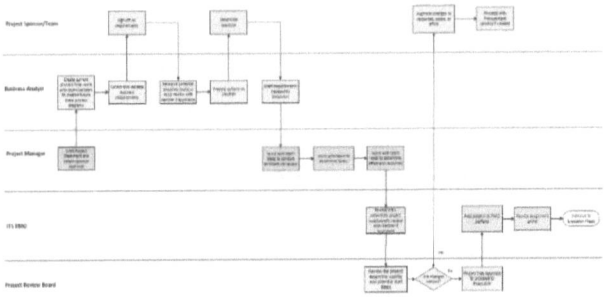

The Project Execution Process
Outputs:
- Weekly Status Update
- Change Management Plan
- Communication Plan
- Testing Plan
- Training Plan

Here I am adding the snapshot of the IT PMO project execution process's overall flow and architecture.

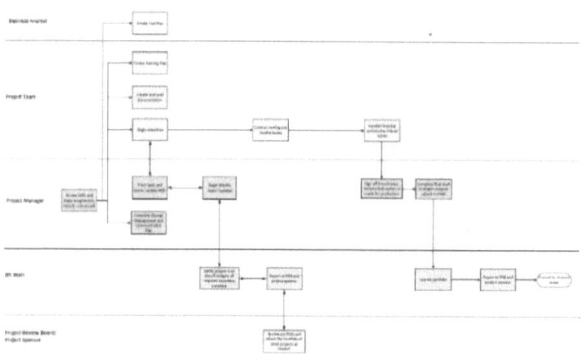

The Project Closeout Process
Outputs:

- Standard Operating Procedure document
- Post-Implementation Evaluation report

Here I am adding the snapshot of the IT PMO project's overall flow and architecture closeout process.

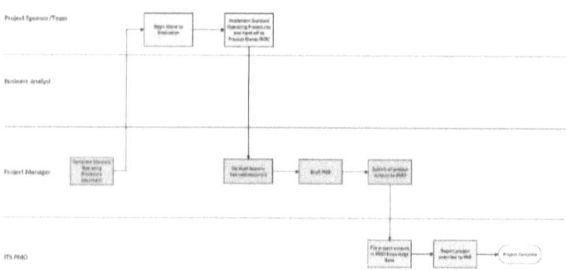

Conclusion

Before we start thinking of setting up the PMO group, it is necessary to ask the following questions.

- What are the objectives and goals of having the PMO group?
- What will be the roles and responsibilities of the PMO group?
- How will the PMO group function?
- Who will be the sponsor of the group?
- What processes, best practices, and governance model the PMO group will follow?

If we have all these answers in place, it will help us define the process, flows, architecture, and roadmap mentioned above. It's not rocket science to set up the PMO group, but it would be equally challenging to have the vision, strategy, goals, and objectives are thoroughly defined before proceeding with the PMO group set up.

Chapter-2

How to create the PMO

Framework

Introduction

As part of my research on "How do we go about getting an effective PMO started?". I have mentioned in my previous chapter some significant ways and process of setting up the PMOs. The next question is what we would do before we could create the PMO roadmap, defined the structure and process flow, so before we could determine these things, we need to finalize the framework that we will be following. Defining and finalizing the framework is the first & foremost aspect of setting up a PMO group. Once we complete our approach, framework, Identify our sponsors, we will then proceed to define roadmap and processes, best-practices, principles, and finalize the tools and applications. Today I will explain what our approach will be in creating the PMO framework? How do we create an effective and efficient framework, which we can rely upon in our present and future? If an organization already has a framework, then how can they reincarnate the same? How the PMO framework restructure will be done when it required to do so? All that I have explained to you in my article today.

Level: -1: Facing the challenge of defining the PMO

The PMO framework's main objective is to form a foundational understanding of PMOs' most common types. To do this, we may need to have a specific set of subject matter experts who have spent much of their professional careers managing, operating, and building different PMOs in different environments, structures, and contexts. All the SME's are have to have a one-day intensive workshop, where the SME's will be working together to develop descriptive frameworks of the most prevalent PMO types. The intent of the workshop should be the followings:

- Identify and reach a consensus on the most common PMO frameworks, which is in practice today.
- Establish and define the variety of PMO practices like domains, enablers, etc.
- Develop a framework profile of each PMO configuration by identifying the practices associated with the PMO's purpose and mission.

The first phase of the framework served as a foundational understanding and was tested with quantifiable measures via a later survey. After the workshop with the SME's, the next step will be to develop PMO configurations, which practitioners could relate to within their context stemming from their day-to-day jobs.

Level: -2: Refining the frameworks

Once the foundational frameworks were completed in level 1, it can be transposed to a brainstorming session. Through the brainstorming session, we can identify and develop the underlying constructs of each Framework. Especially the function and configuration of PMO's refine and our understanding by statistically significant masses. To have a brainstorming session, we will need the people who will operate, manage, and supervise the PMO group, who will sponsor the PMO group, and whom the PMO group will report. The brainstorming session will help identify the framework that will best match the goals, objectives, and mission, and the outcome of the brainstorming session will be in the form of functions, capabilities, and performance related to PMO. Below are the few possible frameworks widely used by several organizations, which are currently in practice.

- *Organization unit PMO/ Business Unit PMO/ Divisional PMO/ Departmental PMO:* Provide project-related services to support a business unit or division within an organization, including, but not limited to, portfolio management, governance, operational project support, and human resource utilization.

- *Project Specific PMO/ Project Office/ Program Office:* Provides project-related services as a temporary entity established to support a specific project or program. May include supporting data management, coordination of governance and reporting, and administrative activities to support project or program team.

- *Project Support/ Services/ Controls Office or PMO:* Provides enabling processes to continuously support the management of the project, program, or portfolio work throughout the organization. They use the governance, processes, best practices, and tools established by the organization. Provide administrative support for the delivery of the project, program, and portfolio work within its domain.

- *Enterprise/ Organization-wide/ Strategic/ Corporate/ Portfolio/ Global PMO:* This is the highest level PMO in an organization. This PMO is often responsible for aligning project and program work to corporate strategy, establishing and ensuring appropriate enterprise governance, and performing portfolio management functions to ensure strategy alignment and benefits realization.
- *Center of Excellence/ Center of Competency:* Supports project work by providing the organization with methodologies, standards, and tools to enable project managers to deliver their projects better. Increase the capability of the organization through acceptable practices and a central point of contact for project managers.

Following are the domain of work, which is usually what a PMO does, and all these aspects can be assessed in the brainstorming session to align these as primary and secondary workstreams.

- *Standards, Methodologies, and Processes:* Methodology definition, Metrics definition, process development, and improvement.
- *Project/ Program delivery management:* Define business goals, resource management, schedule, cost, scope management, business realization management, risk management, stakeholder management, communication, and Project integration.
- *Portfolio Management:* Prioritization, Strategic alignment, Portfolio reporting, Resource management allocation, opportunities, investment analysis, risk management, benefits realization management – Benefits realization structuring, tracking, and reporting.
- *Talent Management:* Provides Training, Career paths, career development, career capability, or skill development, Certifications, career counseling, and enhancements.
- *Governance & Performance Management:* Provides Performance reporting, issue escalation, information distribution, metrics, or KPIs, compliance, financial management, PMO performance management.

- *Organizational Change Management:* Provides Customer, or Stakeholder satisfaction, managing resistance, readiness assessment, stakeholder management, and communication management.
- *Administrative & Support:* Tools – Provisioning, Implementation, support, consulting, and IT/IS support.
- *Knowledge Management:* Define knowledge management policies, managing intellectual collateral/ Property, lessons learned, content management, and collaboration.
- *Strategic Planning:* Confirming strategic priorities, defining business goals, aligning to initiatives, environmental scanning, and opportunity analysis.

Once we are clear on the PMO strategy and framework, it's significant to have a comparative view of all the Frameworks we discussed. The below table is an example of the comparative view of five frameworks widely used across industries. I prepared a few sets of questions, which I usually asked in the brainstorming session to my sponsors and leaders, and based on their answers, I prepared the following output in a table.

I have done the analysis based on the usability of all the frameworks; it covers all the mentioned criteria and the inputs from the brainstorming session and represents the same as an average % value.

It is a sample that I had done for one of my organizations while working on PMO set up. To set the right expectations and get the maximum outputs to finalize the PMO framework, I asked the following questions in the brainstorming session.

1. Which of the following PMO framework will best the organization (all division and global locations)
2. What are the primary & secondary areas that we are focusing on?
3. What are the frequencies of services that we are planning to provide as part of our PMO group? – It will be a multiple option question, and the possible options are routine/ Occasionally/ rarely/ never
4. List all the criteria by which you think your PMO should be evaluated? Or list down the criteria which you feel are or would be the most appropriate for evaluation. Evaluative criteria should be examined individually or in aggregate.
5. To what extent did the PMO focus on external, customer-facing projects, as opposed to projects for internal stakeholders?
6. The Project Management maturity comprises performance within the portfolio, program, and project and the organization's evolution towards an improved state, illustrated by standardizing, measuring, controlling, and improving (SCMI) its performance. So how do you characterize the

project management maturity?

7. What are the different sizes of projects in the pipeline with respect to the budget, which will be part of the PMO group?

8. Any pipeline projects which has a budget above $250k?

9. What is the total estimated value of the projects which were delivered in the past?

10. What was the total estimated financial value (revenue increased, or cost reduction) delivered in the past?

11. Indicate the resource structure of the PMO group, as what will be the contractor and FTE mix?

12. What Percentage of Project managers with PMP, other credentials, and contractors are we planning for?

13. To whom the PMO will report to?

14. How often do you expect the PMO to report the progress?

15. How often would you like to rate the effectiveness of the PMO group? And the rating would be extremely effective, very effective, somewhat effective, not at all effective.

16. Please specify or characterize the PMO group's involvement in each of the phases of strategic management – The answer will be in multiple-choice, i.e., Routinely/ Occasionally/ Rarely/

Never.

17. How would you realize the PMO to contribute business value to the organization – Answer will be in multiple-choice, i.e., Fully realized/ almost realized/ partially realized/ not at all realized.
18. In your past estimation, what percentage of projects completed within the organization that met original goals and business intent?
19. In the past years, within the organization, What percentage of projects completed within their initial budget?
20. In the past year, within the organization, what percentage of projects completed within their initial schedule?
21. Which of these functional areas best describes, to which the PMO will report?

Note: Considering the high performers, we will have to create an algorithm based on the three-performance metrics (80%+ of the project met Original intent, budget, and schedule) to develop a definition of high performers.

ENVISIONING PMO & PROJECT MANAGEMENT THROUGH A JUGGLER'S EYE

Criteria	Study Average	Org Unit PMO	Project Specific	Project Support	EPMO	COE
Customer Mix:						
Internal Stakeholders w/s	48%	47%	42%	46%	53%	47%
External Client Facing	52%	53%	59%	54%	47%	53%
Project Management Maturity:						
High:	14%	11%	24%	17%	15%	16%
Medium:	50%	54%	49%	49%	48%	43%
Low:	36%	35%	27%	42%	37%	41%
Average Number of Project Completed in excess of $250k:	42	40	42	27	51	52
Estimated value of Project completed by PMO:	$100M	$113M	$102M	$81M	$87M	$151M
Estimated Financial Value (revenue/cost reductions) delivered by this PMO:	$71M	$58M	$90M	$64M	$89M	$48M
Number of Employees by Type:						
Project Managers:	16	19	8	17	14	22
Managers:	3	2	3	3	3	3
Project Staff:	26	26	36	21	25	22
Others:	12	14	7	10	6	38
Percentage of Project Managers that are						
PMP credential holders:	43%	43%	38%	35%	55%	63%
Hold other project management certification & credentials:	34%	31%	28%	32%	39%	39%
contract employees:	49%	49%	58%	49%	44%	55%
PMO reports to:						
CEO:	19%	43%	31%	22%	18%	16%
Other C-Suite:	12%	14%	1%	9%	20%	14%
Division VP/ Director:	33%	42%	36%	34%	20%	30%
Reporting frequency of PMO Progress:						
Weekly:	33%	37%	44%	28%	30%	23%
Monthly:	41%	42%	33%	46%	40%	50%
Quarterly:	14%	12%	14%	10%	17%	21%
Number of employees in the organization that the PMO operates:						
<1000:	34%	25%	49%	45%	28%	31%
1000-5000:	25%	29%	14%	24%	30%	22%
5000-50,000:	28%	29%	22%	24%	29%	39%
>50,000:	13%	17%	15%	7%	13%	8%

Highest across Frameworks | Lowest across Frameworks | Highest in that category

Criteria	Study Average	Org Unit PMO	Project Specific	Project Support	EPMO	COE
Routine involvement of PMO in each phase of strategic management:						
Project Implementation:	75%	76%	75%	69%	75%	86%
Project delivery & integration:	62%	66%	65%	56%	62%	74%
Results monitoring & assessment:	61%	61%	64%	64%	66%	60%
Project ID & Prioritization:	49%	49%	50%	43%	57%	50%
Project alignment w/strategic objectives:	42%	37%	37%	33%	58%	40%
Strategy formulation:	32%	26%	39%	28%	43%	24%
PMO's potential to contribute business values to the organization is						
Fully realized:	33%	38%	45%	32%	39%	32%
Partially realized:	62%	62%	51%	61%	63%	54%
not at all realized:	5%	4%	4%	7%	2%	14%
Percentage of projects that successfully met original goals and business intent:	69%	70%	73%	68%	76%	73%
Percentage of projects that finished within their initial budget:	64%	66%	70%	62%	61%	68%
Percentage of projects that finished within their initial scheduled time:	58%	59%	68%	60%	57%	56%
Considered high Performers (80%+of projects met original intent/ budget/ schedule)	19%	18%	20%	17%	25%	24%
PMO's effectiveness in meeting primary purpose						
Extremely effective:	42%	42%	45%	37%	46%	46%
Somewhat effective:	53%	52%	45%	66%	51%	46%
Not at all effective:	5%	6%	10%	4%	3%	8%
Functional reporting area of the PMO (top 3 functions shown)						
PMO:	33%	28%	41%	32%	54%	41%
Operations:	29%	29%	24%	28%	12%	30%
IT or IS:	28%	32%	25%	29%	25%	19%

Highest across Frameworks | Lowest across Frameworks | Highest in that category

Note: The percentage mentioned above has been derived from the output of twenty-one questions asked in the brainstorming session. Based on the answer, I have calculated the average and converted the number to the percentage represented in the above table.

Now that I have explained the steps to have an appropriate PMO framework, but to have a final decision, let us understand the top five frameworks in detail which are used by most of the organizations. Below I have explained all the five frameworks, in fact, along with their criteria. I have also provided the score of each criterion. I have also mentioned the preferred industry, which follows these frameworks.

Organizational Unit PMO/ Business Unit PMO/ Divisional PMO/ Departmental PMO

Description: The organizational unit PMO supports the organizational unit strategy by providing PMO services, including but not limited to portfolio management, governance, operational, and project support to a specific organizational unit. This PMO may provide appropriate information to PMO entities as part of organizational governance and maybe responsible for the consolidated reporting for the Projects, Programs, and portfolios within its domain. There are 54% of organizations that followed this framework.

The below-mentioned tabular analysis has been extracted from the PMI website; as per the PMI research and analysis, Schedule/Cost/ Scope Management has a 77% value addition to an organization if they are proceeding with this PMO group. The sub-criteria is mainly part of "Primary functions performed" by a PMO, so the overall score of each criterion like "Project/Program delivery management"; "Standard, Methodology, processes"; and "Portfolio management prioritization" is what will matter the most to any organization who are planning to have their PMO set up. Likewise, the other two essential functions, i.e., "criteria that PMO is evaluated on" & "primary focus/industry of the PMO," are also considered a similar way. After considering all the key aspects, criteria, and sub-criteria, an organization can decide their PMO framework, which they wanted to use.

Criteria			Value
Primary Functions Performed	Project/ Program Delivery Management	Schedule/Cost/ Scope Management	77%
		Communications	75%
		Resource Management	63%
		Project Integration	60%
		Risk Management	58%
		Overall Score	**46%**
	Standards, Methodology, Processes	Methodology Definition	72%
		Process development and Improvement	69%
		Metrics Definition	51%
		Overall Score	**15%**
	Portfolio Management Prioritization	Portfolio Reporting	66%
		Prioritization	52%
		Resource Management Allocation	49%
		Overall Score	**15%**
Criteria that PMO is evaluated on		Project Delivery v/s Schedule evaluation	75%
		Customer feedback evaluation	68%
		Project cost v/s budget evaluation	65%
		Formal evaluation of Project Managers	56%
		Formal evaluations of PMO staff	54%
Primary focus/industry of the PMO		Information Technology	12%
		Health Care	11%
		Consulting and financial services	10%(each)

Project Specific PMO/ Project Office/ Program Office

Description: The Project-specific PMO provides a range of project and program support services as a temporary entity established to support a specific project or program. These services may include supporting data management, coordination of governance & reporting, and administrative activity to support the project or program team. The group may coordinate with other PMOs to support organizational governance requirements, provide project and program artifacts, and facilitate knowledge management activities. This group usually doesn't exist beyond the life span of a project or program it supports. There are 31% of organizations that followed this framework. The below mentioned tabular analysis has been extracted from the PMI website; as per the PMI research and analysis, Schedule/Cost/ Scope Management is having 91% value addition to an organization if they are proceeding with this PMO group. The sub-criteria is mainly part of "Primary functions performed" by a PMO, so the overall score of each criterion like "Project/Program delivery management"; "Standard, Methodology, processes"; and "Portfolio management prioritization" is what will matter the most to any organization who are planning to have their PMO set up. Likewise, the other two key functions, i.e., "criteria that PMO is evaluated on" & "primary focus/industry of the PMO," are also considered a similar way. After considering all the key aspects, criteria, and Sub-criteria, an organization can decide their PMO framework, which they wanted to use.

Criteria			Value
Primary Functions Performed	Project/ Program Delivery Management	Schedule/Cost/ Scope Management	91%
		Communications	74%
		Resource Management	74%
		Project Integration	71%
		Risk Management	69%
		Overall Score	46%
	Standards, Methodology, Processes	Methodology Definition	87%
		Process development and Improvement	65%
		Metrics Definition	49%
		Overall Score	16%
	Portfolio Management Prioritization	Performance Reporting	74%
		Information distribution	69%
		Issue escalation	69%
		Overall Score	11%
Criteria that PMO is evaluated on		Project Delivery v/s Schedule evaluation	69%
		Project Quality evaluation	68%
		Customer feedback evaluation	68%
		Project cost v/s budget evaluation	63%
		Project Owner feedback evaluation	56%
Primary focus/industry of the PMO		Information Technology	21%
		Consulting	13%
		Telecommunication	11%

Project Support/ Services/ Controls Office or PMO

Description: The Project support office provides enabling processes to support the management of projects, programs, or Portfolio work. It utilizes the governance, processes, best practices, and tools established by the organization and provides administrative support for delivering the project, program, and portfolio work within its domain. If required, it may also develop tools and practices to support a particular project effort specifically. Additionally, it may support mentoring, training, and certification activities for project managers within its area of responsibility. There are 44% of organizations that followed this framework. The below mentioned tabular analysis has been extracted from the PMI website; as per the PMI research and analysis, Schedule/Cost/ Scope Management is having 73% value addition to an organization if they are proceeding with this PMO group. The sub-criteria is mainly part of "Primary functions performed" by a PMO, so the overall score of each criterion like "Project/Program delivery management"; "Standard, Methodology, processes"; and "Portfolio management prioritization" is what will matter the most to any organization who are planning to have their PMO set up. Likewise, the other two key functions, i.e., "criteria that PMO is evaluated on" & "primary focus/industry of the PMO," are also considered a similar way. After considering all the key aspects, criteria, and sub-criteria, an organization can decide their PMO framework, which they wanted to use.

		Criteria	Value
Primary Function Performed	Project/Program Delivery Management	Schedule/Cost/Scope Management	73%
		Communications	73%
		Resource Management	48%
		Project Integration	69%
		Risk Management	60%
		Overall Score	**47%**
	Standards, Methodology, Processes	Methodology Definition	66%
		Process development and Improvement	69%
		Metrics Definition	46%
		Overall Score	**19%**
	Portfolio Management Prioritization	Portfolio Reporting	51%
		Risk Management	46%
		Prioritization	41%
		Overall Score	**12%**
Criteria that PMO is evaluated on		Project Delivery v/s Schedule evaluation	77%
		Customer feedback evaluation	63%
		Project cost v/s budget evaluation	63%
		Formal evaluation of Project Managers	55%
		Stakeholder feedback evaluation	48%
Primary focus/Industry of the PMO		Information Technology	22%
		Government	16%
		Manufacturing	15%

Enterprise/ Organization-wide/ Strategic/ Corporate/ Portfolio/ Global PMO

Description: The Enterprise PMO is the highest level PMO entity in an organization, often responsible for the alignment of project and program work to corporate strategy, establishing & ensuring appropriate enterprise project, program & portfolio governance, performing portfolio management functions to ensure strategy alignment & benefits realization, and responsible for the alignment of initiatives to corporate strategy. The EPMO may facilitate governance at the enterprise level and may incorporate strategy development and strategy planning support. The EPMO may have direct responsibility or may influence other lower-level PMO's. Management of multiple stakeholders and ensuring continuous communication are the critical roles of the EPMO. There are 39% of organizations that followed this framework. The below mentioned tabular analysis has been extracted from the PMI website; as per the PMI research and analysis, Schedule/Cost/ Scope Management is having 73% value addition to an organization if they are proceeding with this PMO group. The sub-criteria is mainly part of "Primary functions performed" by a PMO, so the overall score of each criterion like "Project/Program delivery management"; "Standard, Methodology, processes"; and "Portfolio management prioritization" is what will matter the most to any organization who are planning to have their PMO set up.

Likewise, the other two key functions, i.e., "criteria that PMO is evaluated on" & "primary focus/industry of the PMO," are also considered a similar way. After considering all the key aspects, criteria, and sub-criteria, an organization can decide their PMO framework, which they wanted to use.

	Criteria		Value
Primary Functions Performed	Project/ Program Delivery Management	Schedule/Cost/ Scope Management	73%
		Communications	71%
		Resource Management	48%
		Project Integration	67%
		Risk Management	63%
		Overall Score	**30%**
	Standards, Methodology, Processes	Methodology Definition	80%
		Process development and Improvement	74%
		Metrics Definition	52%
		Overall Score	**20%**
	Portfolio Management Prioritization	Portfolio Reporting	77%
		Prioritization	65%
		Strategic Alignment	65%
		Overall Score	**25%**
Criteria that PMO is evaluated on		Project Delivery v/s Schedule evaluation	74%
		Customer feedback evaluation	68%
		Project cost v/s budget evaluation	62%
		Performance against the financial goal	57%
		Stakeholder feedback evaluation	57%
Primary focus/industry of the PMO		Financial Services	21%
		Information Technology	14%
		Government	11%

Center of Excellence/ Center of Competency

Description: The center of excellence supports the execution of project work by equipping the organization with methodology, standards, and tools to enable project managers to deliver the projects better.

The Center of Excellence increases the organization's capability by implementing good practices and providing a central point of contact for project managers. It may also provide mentoring, training, and capability development for people and facilitate knowledge management through knowledge capture and information distribution. There are 35% of organizations that followed this framework. The below-mentioned tabular analysis has been extracted from the PMI website; as per the PMI research and analysis, Schedule/Cost/ Scope Management has a 51% value addition to an organization if they are proceeding with this PMO group. The sub-criteria is mainly part of "Primary functions performed" by a PMO, so the overall score of each criterion like "Project/Program delivery management"; "Standard, Methodology, processes"; and "Portfolio management prioritization" is what will matter the most to any organization who are planning to have their PMO set up. Likewise, the other two key functions, i.e., "criteria that PMO is evaluated on" & "primary focus/industry of the PMO," are also considered a similar way. After considering all the key aspects, criteria, and sub-criteria, an organization can decide their PMO framework, which they wanted to use.

Criteria			Value
Primary Functions Performed	Project/Program Delivery Management	Schedule/Cost/Scope Management	51%
		Communications	50%
		Resource Management	44%
		Project Integration	44%
		Risk Management	49%
		Overall Score	24%
	Standards, Methodology, Processes	Methodology Definition	72%
		Process development and improvement	84%
		Metrics Definition	56%
		Overall Score	41%
	Portfolio Management Prioritization	Defining business goals & alignment	27%
		Confirming strategic priorities	25%
		Opportunity Analysis	22%
		Overall Score	14%
Criteria that PMO is evaluated on		Project Delivery v/s Schedule evaluation	69%
		Customer feedback evaluation	69%
		Project cost v/s budget evaluation	59%
		Formal evaluations of PMO staff	69%
		Internal demand for PMO services	56%
Primary focus/industry of the PMO		Government	16%
		Manufacturing	14%
		Energy	14%

Conclusion

I have done PMO framework research in 2012, 2015, and 2019. In each of these years, I have identified these five frameworks mentioned above. The research is mainly done to identify the different configurations of PMO's, i.e., frameworks, to learn about their respective missions, goals, objectives, how they are structured, how they operate, and what they look like. This essential step will lay out a basic understanding of PMO structure, landscape, and address questions raised by mid-to-upper-level management responsible for developing, reincarnating, implementing, and managing PMO. Furthermore, by aligning performance metrics in the delivery of business value, the research and analysis will help determine which PMO frameworks can be more productive through their methods, services, and processes.

This analysis will further provide PMO directors and managers with the ability to:
- Compare the PMO with the closest matching framework to benchmark against important services and performance criteria.
- Learn about the best standard practices across all the PMO frameworks and the higher-performing PMOs.

With this, PMO managers will be better positioned to reengineer their provision of services and support for executing an organization's portfolio of projects and strategic initiatives.

Chapter-3

Key PMO Roles and Responsibilities

Introduction

The project management model is evolving vigorously. Given the impact of unsettling forces of change have on the nature of work and demand for resources; it's no surprise why offices associated across the globe wish for consistency. While the truth is stranger than fiction, Project Management Blends reported that setting up a Program Management Office enabled larger firms to deliver their projects within budget & time.

The need to deliver value in times of vagueness is increasing. So, an organization needs to understand a project management office's roles and responsibilities before they could set up their Project Management Office.

The Project Management Office is a central body that can be externally or internally set up with a set of dedicated team, budget, and mission. Primarily, PMO builds the plan, sets the baseline, and create a roadmap for the business. PMO also standardizes processes, procedures, and methodologies to align the Project portfolio to business objectives. This article will take a quick look at a PMO's responsibilities and the challenges it addresses.

Key PMO Responsibilities

A Project Management Office is liable for establishing guidelines and frameworks for Project managers and business units to adhere to them. They audit projects in a program and profile feasibility based on time, data, costs, and resources. By doing this, it will ensure that multiple projects can run in a repeatable and supportable manner. The corporate PMO has sovereignty over functions and provides a skilled workforce that is assigned work, which makes optimal use of niche competencies experiential prowess. Some of the PMO tasks and responsibilities are the followings:

1. *Establishing Governance:* This is one of the critical PMO function and one of the primary PMO function. By establishing governance, PMO ensures the right people can access the right and relevant information to bring in strategic decisions. It involves teams, stakeholders, investors, and clients on change management policies to facilitate a seamless evolution when new leadership takes over the organization's leads. Once role-based assignments are clarified, then projects stand a chance of continuing the path.

2. *Resource Management:* Managing resources is an essential aspect of the PMO process because the right resources are crucial to delivering high-visibility and high-return projects. Having them onboarded before the pipeline projects commence would be on every PMO manager's purview. It's the PMO's responsibility to see that organizational resources are optimally shared across projects. In short, a pool of competent resources, skills, and their bandwidth are tallies against their current and future availability to prevent the misstep in project planning.

3. *Reusability:* The PMO enables team efficiency by allowing collaborative knowledge transfers between departmental project teams. PMO group makes Project plans, reviews, templates, and documentation widely available to respective members and available to be used across the organizations. It saves time that would have otherwise gone into rework. Rather than reinventing the wheel, project teams can not only reduce their learning curve but can also get more work off the ground from the organizational knowledge being shared.

4. *Mentor and train Project Managers:* The Project management office provide support, mentoring, and coaching to project managers. After all, the project managers are the heart of the project life cycle. Developing a project manager's competencies enhances their ability to lead and manage project execution and team dynamics. Mentoring and coaching project managers will equip them to gauge their team's strengths and prevent conflict between members. This way, the project can tap into potential from within, with staff whose essential skills and knowledge can be used to complete tasks and help one another out.

5. *Track and Support Projects:* The Project Management office doesn't make conclusive decisions; it offers those with a vested interest in the portfolio, i.e., key decision-makers. It tracks project health by ascertaining dependencies between projects. The Project Management Office relies on a project-portfolio management strategy to assess all the completed projects. It collects and collates cyclic updates on the work breakdown structures, communication strategy, and registered risks. The next step it takes to implement a remedial program to prevent issues from becoming recurring risks.

6. *Provide Reporting Function:* One of the core PMO services involves collecting data about project progress, the status of milestones, goals reached, etc. The report captured the project's health and provided perceptions into processes and frameworks that work. It centralizes information and supports a balanced scorecard for projects. It examines operational efficiency and compares the financial performance against a project's return on investment and non-financial benefits. Additionally, it saves operational costs and effort in looking up critical information during a time crunch.

How are PMO teams structured?

The PMO team is headed by a PMO leader who is adept at shifting strategies. In other words, as a new opportunity come up and is brought to the project leader's attention, then the onus is on the project leader to ascertain its long-term benefits and how it affiliates best with business goals. Team members are chosen based on their awareness of the project environments and experiential seniority within the industry. Typically, the project management offices comprise the followings:

1. *Director:* A Project director is generally a former project manager with years of practical experience

managing and delivering projects.

2. *Project Sponsor:* The Chief personnel who weighs the pros and cons of taking up a project scopes it out and subsequently confines it to a realistic timebox.
3. *Business Analysts:* A team of business analysts relies on data analysis to deepen their learning of the portfolio, providing answers to questions relating to the feasibility of the projects and benefits promised.
4. *Service Delivery Managers:* Also known as program delivery managers, they have the expertise of rolling out services. They are in the know of reskilling and upskilling measures that keep project teams employable and relevant.
5. *Project Manager:* A crucial resource that leads and manages projects and teams. They take ownership of multiple projects and formulate strategies to realize the project's promised benefits.

Conclusion

It would be better to be staffed with people who know their roles and know how to get the right resources to play to their strengths to support the PMO's administration, function, and capabilities. Mastering the essentials of resource management software can also prove beneficial.

It can provide unmatched visibility and insights into existing workflows, ensuring no competent resource falls through the cracks. And most importantly, it considers incoming demands and lets you plan out the acquisition and deployment of sufficient workforce capacity.

Chapter-4

What is Project Governance and The Process to Create an Effective Governance Framework

What is Governance?
According to Wikipedia, the definition of governance is the process whereby elements in society wield power, authority, influence, and enact policies & decisions concerning public life, economic and social development."

Definition of Project Governance, according to Wikipedia, is the management framework within which project decisions are made. Project governance is a critical element of any project since the accountabilities and responsibilities associated with an organization's business as usual activities are laid down in their organizational governance arrangements.

So here is what I like to define project governance in simple terms: Governance is nothing but to establish policies, processes, and best practices and to monitor their implementation continuously by a group of people (governing body) in an organization.

We will include the mechanism required to balance the power of the members and their primary duty of enhancing the prosperity and viability of the organization.

What is the purpose of having governance?

The purpose of having a governance model is to provide a decision-making framework, which is logical, robust, and repeatable to govern any activity and independent of underlying usage of organizational best practices and methodologies. An organization will have a structured approach for conducting its business as usual, and business change through this.

Governance will formalize a what-if scenario in case of issue management (like budget restriction and any unforeseen events), decision management. The governance model will help in resolving the uncertainties and provide clarity for the roles of all designated and defined stakeholders.

Here is a representation of good governance and its benefits

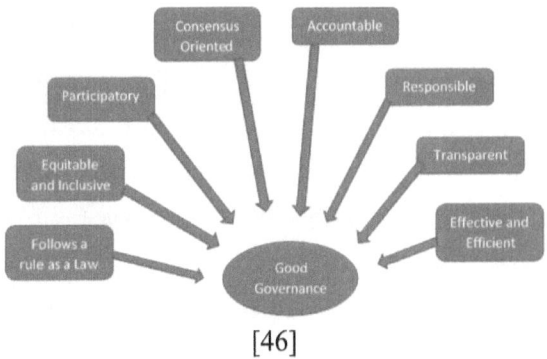

Principles for creating an effective governance framework

Good governance is always supported by a set of principles, which will guide them. Here are certain principles that will help to create an effective and productive governance model.

Principle: -1: Assure a single point of accountability for success: The Concept of a Single point of accountability is the first principle of effective and productive project governance, as every project required a leader to assure success. The right person must be made accountable and either endorsed or empowered by the senior leaders to have sufficient authority within the organization.

Principle: -2: Separate Project Ownership from the stakeholders: It is significant for a project manager to define a project stakeholder map for all the stakeholders and a specific governance structure for a formal decision process along with the project life cycle. The only mechanism to ensure that projects meet their customer and stakeholders' needs while optimizing the cost is to allocate the project owner as a specialist party, who will not be a stakeholder to the project. The Project owner is engaged in a precise term that outlines the organization's key result areas and the organization's critical stakeholders' views.

Generally, organizations establish a project committee's governance, which identifies projects' existence and appoints project owners as early as possible in a project life cycle. The project committee also establishes a project council that oversees the project progress, performance, and ensures the project's key result area is consistent with the organization's values. These parameters are generally included in the governance plan, and they remain in place for the life of a project from a project management plan. The project may have many stakeholders, and an effective governance framework may address their needs.

Principle:-3: Ensure the Project stakeholder management and project decision-making activity are separate and distinct: The committee's decision-making effectiveness can be inversely proportional to its size. A larger committee failed to make a timely decision. When project decision-making forums grow in size, they tend to morph into stakeholder management groups. When the number increases, the detailed understanding of each of the attendees on critical project issues reduces. Usually, few of the stakeholders attend not to make any decisions, but a way to determine what is happening in the project. Not because these stakeholders do not have sufficient time to make their point, but they have to compete with time and influence with those who have peripheral involvement in the project.

Moreover, all the stakeholders will not have a similar understanding of the critical project issue, so sometimes bringing everyone to speed up can be a waste of time.

Hence, more significant project committees are constituted more as a stakeholder management forum than a decision-making forum. It usually happens when a project is dependent on the committee to make a timely decision. Both the activities, stakeholder management, and decision-making are significant in every project's success. Still, we will have to remember that these are two separate activities and have to be treated the same way. If this separation can be achieved, it will help you avoid clogging the decision-making by constraining its members to only those selected stakeholders. They are critical for the project's success. It may further lead to the problem of disgruntled stakeholders considers that their needs are not being considered. The project stakeholder mechanism should address this concern as it will help you capture the needs, views, and inputs of all your stakeholders and address them to their satisfaction.

Principle:-4: Ensure Separation of Project governance and organizational governance structure: The project governance structure is established because the organization's governance can't be able to suffice the necessary framework to deliver the project and ensure it's a success. Project governance should be in line with the organization's governance structure, but it can't be treated as a single governance structure.

The project required flexibility, speed of decision making, and hierarchical mechanism, and it can't be associated with traditional organizational structure. Consequently, the project governance framework established for a project should remain separate from the organizational structure. It's recognized that organizations have valid requirements in terms of reporting and stakeholder involvement. However, the project's reporting mechanism can address the former, and the project governance framework must address the latter.

Approaches to create a Governance model/ framework

When creating a governance framework, it's significant to think about what approach we will follow to create an effective governance framework. Here I have mentioned the approaches to create an effective governance framework.

We can take a three-part approach to define or establishing new governance and operating model or enhancing an existing model. These approaches suggest that organizations and their leaders form a governance model and delegate the activity to the appropriate parties to carry it out in a unique manner. Let's discuss these three parts.

Part-1: Define the operating requirement or look for a framework that will best suit your organization, or you can design your operating framework for your governance model. Factor in any regulatory, governance, or legal requirements that are applicable and in line with your organization's governance model. Define and consider the scope of your operation and how do you factor them in your model. Understand your organization's governance model and its strengths and weaknesses.

Part-2: Design the governance operating model and all its components. Define Key responsibilities, accountabilities, decision rights, and escalation paths.

Part-3: Implement your governance operating model. The model should define how your board and your organization will measure success using standards, best practices, and metrics. The model should combine governance requirements, organizational functions, and business requirements to allocate resources accordingly. The implementation of the governance operating model should also recommend how frequently the organization or its board will review the governance model. Organizations may engage the third party to do the governance model review. The review process will include the components, the plan, and the implementation of a governance model.

Tasks and Elements of Governance

While creating a governance framework, we need to consider the following tasks and elements, which will help us to create an effective governance framework.

- Project governance will outline the relationships between internal and external groups involved in a project.
- Describe the proper flow of information regarding the project to all the stakeholders.
- Ensure the appropriate review of issues identified within the project.
- Ensure the required approval and direction for the project is obtained at each appropriate stage of the project.

Elements to be included to have a good governance framework/ structure.

To create an effective governance framework, we must include the following critical tasks and elements.
- To have a business case with clearly defined objectives of a project. It should also have to specify

In-scope & out-scope aspects.
- Creates the mechanism to assess the compliance of a project to its original objective.
- Identifying all the stakeholders and understanding their level of interest in the project.
- Set up a clear and robust communication plan.
- Set of business-level requirements as agreed by stakeholders.
- An agreed specification for the project delivery
- The appointment of a Project Manager
- Clear assignment of Project roles and responsibility
- The project plans
- Status reporting
- Create a document repository for the project
- Create a glossary for the project
- The process to provide issue management
- The process to provide communication and Risk management
- Create a standard process for quality review of the key governance documents and the project deliverables.

Presentation of tasks and elements of project governance with a role play

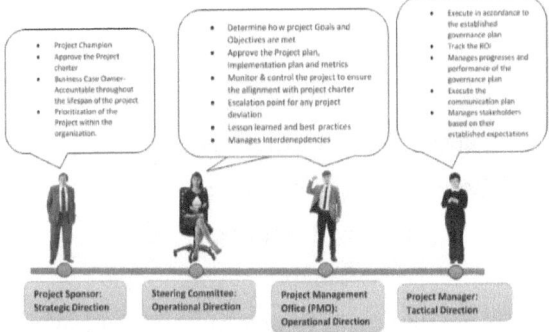

Why is project governance critical to the success of a project?

Establishing good project governance is often a daunting task, as it required significant investment when embarking on a new project. It is sometimes challenging to define the benefits when it comes to investing in the creation of a project governance framework. Here are four key benefits of creating project governance:

- Single point of accountability
- Outlining the roles, responsibility, and relationship among project stakeholders

- Information dissemination and transparent communication

- Issue management and resolution

Conclusion

Project Governance provides a single point of accountability. It mandates clarity and consistency of decision making throughout the life span of a project, and this doesn't mean that "one throat to choke." Still, one person will be responsible for the project's direction and focus, and having multiple individuals accountable will not blur this. Besides this, project governance defines and clearly articulates structured roles, responsibilities, and accountabilities within the project. This helps in making a timely decision; this comes to play when a project manager has a deviation in scope, budget, time, resources, quality, or even when a risk crops up. Then the project governance defines whom these will impact and how to deal with the impact. The governance framework provides a guideline on how to deal with the impact. Not only this, but it also details the mechanism for how to deal with the issue. The governance framework ensures that the appropriate review on the issue is done and who are the key point of contact for addressing and approving any deviation in the project. Project governance provides direction, defines decision-making procedures and metrics for validating impacts in the project. It also empowers the project team to deliver the requirements and create a forum for issue resolution to occur on time. Lastly, project governance provides a vehicle for information gatherings ad reporting to all stakeholders.

The governance framework ensures that the communication plan is well defined, updated, and executed. It also facilitates consistent, standardized, and transparent reporting. The governance framework promotes nibble status updates on productivity as well as communicates and addresses stakeholder's expectations.

Reference:
https://insights.diligent.com/corporate-governance/how-to-build-a-strong-governance-model#:~:text=Governance%20models%20should%20establish%20the,clear%20to%20employees%20and%20stakeholders.

Chapter-5

Process of developing a PMO strategic Plan

Introduction

Strategic level PMOs are also known as enterprise project management offices. They are essential in developing, maintaining, and communicating effective project programs and portfolio practices. Having an organization-wide strategic plan provides a blueprint for all PMO initiatives to be aligned with and measured against it. As per my recent research, I realized that only 40-45% of strategic PMOs have a high level of alignment with their organization's strategy. In the current vastly changing time, organizations are under tremendous pressure to develop a PMO strategic plan.

The Beginning

If PMO or EPMO doesn't have a strategic plan that aligns with overall operational goals, then projects are at risk of ruining resources and time and are unlikely to produce the desired results. It is critical that organizations' first identity is to create a long-term operational goals, establish a PMO, and then develop a PMO strategic plan, which aligns with organizational goals and objectives.

Process

Here are some criteria that will help organizations develop a PMO strategic plan, which utilizes talents, technologies, and resources to synchronize activities with business goals and objectives and improve overall organizational performance.

Establish an understanding of the organization's vision and mission: Without having a clear understanding of the organization's vision, mission, and goals, it's nearly impossible to establish a successful PMO plan. To get a holistic picture of an organization's overall strategic vision, mission, and goals, PMO leaders should be directly involved in the executive planning sessions at a strategic level. It is the way where a PMO can be useful in their approach and endeavors.

Establish and prioritize PMO goals: PMO leaders and the c-suite executives should work together to identify company-wide objectives and determine PMO's role in meeting them. All goals and objectives should be directly linked with the higher-level organization's initiatives instead of focusing on department-level projects. Identification of goals and prioritizing each resulting project should be a coordinated effort between executives and the PMO leadership team.

Assess PMO resources and capabilities: To develop an effective strategic plan, all available resources, including internal and outsourced resources, must be assessed. PMO leaders should examine the PMOs' capabilities and technologies to determine their PMOs' strengths and weaknesses. By doing so, PMO leaders can advocate for the right type and amount of resources to sufficiently and adequately support an organization's goals and objectives without the risk of gaps, which can impact the PMOs' ability to deliver the results. It is a vital step for securing the full buy-in from the c-suite executives or Sr. Leaders. Without having the full backing of the executive team, or the necessary people, processes, and technology, the PMO simply cannot effectively execute any strategic plan.

Document the PMOs plan to connect the goals, objectives and reduce risks: Once full buy-in and support for the PMO is received from the executive team, PMO leaders can start formalizing a strategic plan. The plan must include the followings: organization's vision, mission, and goals, the role of the PMO and how it intends to execute projects in a way which can accomplish company-wide goals, and objective, the available resources and how they will be utilized, strategies for dealing with factors which may impact outcomes, and the success of the PMO will be measured.

Monitor and measure performance: Establish relevant PMO performance indicators to measure success. It is vital to have KPIs defined to measure the success in determining whether PMO has been strategically effective or not. These indicators will help identify where the PMO may be deficient and where corrections and assistance may be necessary. It can isolate issues in various areas such as human resources, processes, budget, quality control, and how technologies are being leveraged. Apart from identifying the gaps, KPIs will help the PMO identify organizational impacts to adjust their strategic plan accordingly. The PMO has no other option than KPIs to determine whether their plan is on track and to catch the red flag early to avoid more significant problems.

Recommend changes and improvement: It not sufficient to identify the performance shortfalls. A strategic plan can only be successful if PMO leaders recognize, recommend, and implement improvements to increase the chances of meeting the organization's goals and objectives. All recommendations should be vetted with the executive team to ensure all key considerations have been factored in. Final approval should also be received from executives, as changes to the strategic plan will also impact the company as a whole.

Implement approved changes: Not all the recommend changes or improvements will get approval from the organization's leaders. It makes sense to implement some changes immediately while others are more appropriate to implement in the future. It's necessary to prioritize and ensure the correct time to implement changes before executing them.

Assess changes as needed: The PMO strategic plan should be reassessed as company-wide goals, hierarchy, resources, policy, or other changes might have an impact on the success or failure of the PMO. Many different factors can play a vital role like regulatory hurdles, changes in key personnel, cultural shift, and a host of other things. That is why change management specialists should be consulted to ensure nothing should fall through the cracks.

Develop and maintain a culture of excellence and accountability: All the members of PMO plays a critical role in maintaining a high standard of excellence. It happens through accountability, whereby each member understands and recognizes the significance of their work in contributing to or detracting from overall team performance.

Conclusion

The mentioned process to develop a strategic PMO plan that can help organizations ensure the PMO is more effective and better prepared to achieve organization-wide goals and objectives. It will also ensure that the Sr. leaders and c-suite executives are supporting their PMOs, which is very necessary for a PMO to sustain and survive. If the PMO of an organization survives, sustains, and delivers the desired results in a critical time, it can take the organization to a newer height of success.

Chapter-6

Tips for Managing the Project Budget

Introduction
Budget overruns are like the litmus test for project success or failure. Some of the companies may have an unlimited budget, but some have a limited and structured budget allocated for each of their business units. The first thing project stakeholders should look to determine whether their project was a great success or a colossal failure is a bottom line. This fact fuels the pressure for the Project leaders, and their teams face with each passing day. As like effective budget management is the primary area of focus for the project managers who value their careers. I have mentioned a few strategies that can help control the project budget before it succumbs to whopping cost overruns.

Understand the requirements and wants of the Stakeholders
The Stakeholder requirement or what they wanted in a project

often isn't simple as it may seem upfront. It can lead to unidentified goals and expectations on both sides of a coin. If the project managers, sponsors, team members, and vendors don't have a solid grasp on the stakeholder's requirements, it will become difficult to define the project requirements.

Be sure to invest as much time as required to get a deeper understanding of what the stakeholders expect. The zest of a project, including the budget, is defined after understanding stakeholders' expectations. To manage the project budget effectively, we need to have the project deliverables, accurately defined & documented project requirements, clearly defined stakeholders requirements, and agreement of stakeholders on the project requirements. All the mentioned steps should be completed before the project budget is set. There are many projects where budget overruns. The reason behind it is that it could have been initiated around the needs and executed around the wants.

Budget for Surprises

It is good to be realistic when it comes to estimating the cost of a project. Ensure to get an estimate from all the applicable and required stakeholders and, more importantly, build contingencies. Some of the organizations may ask their project managers to build in the exact and accurate cost plan and estimates, but being a project manager adding up contingency should come naturally. While creating a cost estimate, it's wise to factor in the things which is beyond the project manager's control. External environmental considerations may impact the pricing of supplies, resources, labor, financing, product/service shortages, currency exchange, etc. The prices which a project manager enquires today may not carry through to the later stage of a project.

So, it's good to ensure that vendors should deliver as per their promises on the agreements. It is always virtuous to have a back-up plan in such a case. Getting inputs from other stakeholders and vetting suppliers and vendors can help a project manager travel the distance of setting up a more realistic budget. It can be easily met and to address all the unforeseen circumstances that can potentially impact the project budget.

Developing relevant KPIs

To manage a project budget effectively, one needs to establish the key performance indicators (KPIs). KPIs help you to ascertain how much budget has been spent on a project. KPI's help to find out as to what extent the project budget differs from what was planned. Here are some of the KPIs which are very common and widely used across the organizations.

- ***Actual Cost:*** It is also known as the actual cost of work performed (ACWP); it shows how much money spent on a project to date.
- ***Cost Variance:*** Indicates whether the estimated project cost is above or below the set baseline.
- ***Earned Value:*** It is known as the budgeted cost of

work performed (BCWP); it shows the approved budget for all the performed project activities up to a particular time

- ***Planned Value:*** It is known as the budgeted cost of work scheduled (BWCS); it is the estimated cost for project activities that are planned/scheduled as of the reporting date.
- Return on investment (ROI): This shows a project's profitability and whether the benefits have exceeded the costs.

Revisit, Review & Re-forecast

When a project is executed without proper budget management and re-forecasting, then such projects are prone to the fiasco. Frequent budget oversight is vital in preventing budgets from getting too far out of the project manager's hand. A ten percent budget overrun is far easier to correct than a fifty percent budget overrun. So, when the project managers ignore the project budget and re-forecast, then the ten percent overrun can quickly become fifty percent overrun. It's better to review a project budget periodically and frequently than forecasting it and then pay attention to the budget when it goes beyond the control. Just like the project budget needs to be continuously revisited to keep it on track, the resource usage needs to be continuously revisited because the resources working on a project contribute to its cost. So, an ideal project should review the number of resources currently working on a task as well as the future resource need on a weekly/ bi-weekly basis.

Checking resource requirements regularly and periodically ensures that the resources are fully utilized, and the project team is ready with the right set of resources for the rest of the project. Apart from all these aspects, scope creep is another aspect that causes the budget overrun. All the unplanned work will always find its way to fit into the project approved scope. It, in return, mount the billable hours, which will have a direct impact on the project budget. So, it is advised that a project manager carefully manage the project's scope by creating change requests for the work that were not part of the initial requirements, and all these change requests authorize additional funding for the project to cover the extra work. Thus, it keeps a project aligned with the new budget.

Defining RACI and sharing the responsibility and accountability

Defining RACI metrics and sharing the responsibility and accountability equally among the project team members will reduce the burden on Project managers, and it ensures that all the key parties are well aware of the project budget. It is only an essential aspect of conflict management, but it can help a project staying on budget. It is wise for a project manager to inform the project team of the budget forecast because a knowledgeable team is an empowered team that takes ownership of its projects.

A project team is more likely to watch their project charges and be less likely to charge extra grey-area hours (hours they know they worked, but the resources weren't clear about what they were working on) to the project informed about the budget status.

Conclusion

The Project budget is a living part of a project. It gives breathing space to a project manager, and it helps a project manager to demonstrate their real skills and expertise. In an ideal case, the project managers who stay on top of their project budget and track every moving and dull piece of the budget are more likely to keep their sponsors, stakeholders, and management happy.

Chapter-7

Aligning Project Management with Business Strategy

Introduction

Project Management office professionals hold significant knowledge that can help in ensuring alignment for businesses focused on achieving their vision. For organizations of today to reach their full operational effectiveness, C-suites should need to unlock the potentials of their PMO resources. Many PMOs were set up to manage and meet program and project-specific deliverables and requirements and did not necessarily have a substantial direct link with high-level business objectives. In today's disruptive time, PMOs' effectiveness is increasingly measured by how they can be able to map a direct link to the success of overall business performance.

Uncovered Potentials
The PMO should play a vital role in ensuring that business

objectives are successfully met. The days are gone when PMO's are only enthralled to manage a project and program-specific outcomes.

The following issues may arise when a PMO lacks alignment with the business strategy.

Ambiguous PMO direction: In my recent research, I found out that 80-90% of senior executives believe activities that support strategic goals are pivotal to keeping up the changing economic conditions. However, most of the C-Suites and senior executives are unclear on how to accomplish such a daunting task. According to PMI's survey for benefits realization management framework, only 5-10% of the organizations were successful in meeting their strategic goals. The main problem is that PMO resources are utilized to focus primarily on project success, not on the strategic objectives.

Underutilized PMO resources: PMOs are mainly set up in a business unit level formation and not focused on organization-wide performance as a whole. In my recent article on the PMO framework, I have mentioned the percentage of usability of PMO types. So, departmental/ business unit based PMO is being used by 54% or organizations, and project-specific PMO is being used by 44% of organizations. It shows that the majority of the organization's focus is on Project success rather than strategic alignment.

Low company performance at a high cost: As per my previous article, I have mentioned only 39% of organizations used enterprise PMO, so which means only 39% of the businesses are aligned with their strategy. Yet, the cost of the PMO's is on the rise. Organizations should always remember that a PMO is a valuable resource, and their activities should be supporting the organizations' high-level plans and vision. Implementing only soiled departmental projects is the reflection of the ineffective use of human and financial resources. So, C-Suites and Senior leaders should be focusing more on maximizing these assets.

A decline in Project success rates: In the current disruptive time, we all know that the PMO growth is on the rise, but if we compare the growth rate with its success rate, then we will realize that the success rate of projects is declining. Lack of aligning PMOs with business strategy is the primary reason behind this failure.

Benefits of Strategic Alignment
PMOs that ensuring alignment with strategic objectives, goals, and vision are almost twice as likely to become high-

performing teams capable of implementing successful strategies and creating significant values. High-performing PMOs are four times more likely than low-performers to execute planned strategy.

They are also three times more likely to be successful in enabling companies to perform financially. The organizations must consider transitioning their traditional business unit/ departmental/ Project-specific PMOs to an enterprise project management office (EPMO), which focuses on executing projects in alignment with overall business strategy. If we have to follow the statistical data, then according to PMI, EPMOs are capable of improving portfolio reporting by 20%, strategic alignment services by 23%, confirming strategic priorities, and project alignment with strategic objectives both by 10%.

Transforming to an EPMO

In my article "Transformational PMO's & its characteristics," I have explained transformational PMO and its characteristics in detail. So, it would be wise for the organizations to prepare their PMOs to transform into an EPMO model in the current disruptive time. It will help them keep pace with the increasing competition and ensure that strategic objectives are met throughout the project lifecycles. I have mentioned the characteristics and the recommendations of transforming a

PMO in my article dated on 18th Aug-2020, so kindly refer to the same for more details. Overall, when an organization is preparing to transform into an EPMO, they focus primarily on the following.

Planning and Initiation: Business needs to consider setting up their EPMO for ensuring all business units are undertaking initiatives that tie to overall strategic goals. The EPMO participation is vital in organization-wide planning sessions for successfully transforming their traditional PMOs into a high-performing team, which delivers significant values. This process will help to establish a shared vision across the organization.

Monitoring activities, resources, and performance: The EPMO leaders and Senior executives must work closely together to maintain alignment between projects and overall business goals during the project implementations. The EPMO and senior leaders should include establishing key performance indicators to communicate and measure their organizations' matters the most.

Conclusion

At the end of the projects, It is significant for the PMOs and senior executives to quantify all their projects' success rate with organization-wide objectives and determine what changes are required for future projects to help their business sustain and grow in the right direction. Gaining an understanding of lessons learned is the sure-shot formula for success.

To achieve this together, the senior executives should consider their EPMO as their strategic partners, which reports directly to the executive team, and not solely a project-based business unit. If the PMOs are only restricted to a Project-based business unit, then it becomes more difficult for an organization to compete, and the stakeholders will continue to expect more from all areas of businesses. To ensure the PMOs to become exceptionally efficient and effective, they should be allowed to modify contributions. In short, an organization, C-Suites, will have to prepare their EPMOs to transform into a high-performing team. It will enable the EPMOs to keep up with changing economic conditions, and C-Suits should work closely with their EPMOs to develop activities that support strategy and raise the success rate or an organization-wide project.

Chapter-8

Project Managers - Are they, Warriors or Bookkeepers

Introduction

There is a trend in the business that is disturbing: Mostly, companies are recruiting for project managers who are PMP certified while ignoring the actual traits and experience which demonstrate successful project management skills and abilities. Sometimes PMP certifications can be contra-indicators of a project manager's essential skills because their focus might not be on managing projects but rather on managing the process of a project. I have seen the leaders showing up to save a failing project to find exceptional project documentation, project plans, and paperwork in my career. But still, the leaders can't answer with confidence even the most basic questions like "Are you going to go-live on Schedule"? Even I have heard the statements like all managers are project managers combined with an apparent lack of appreciation of the difference between a project coordinator role and a project manager. To clarify that all managers are task managers, they do not possess project management skills, and they are rarely project managers. Project coordinators are administrators, not managers.

Project Management is not just Project Administration.

Generally, project managers come in two primary flavors. First is the bookkeeper. These PMs document the indefinite detail on progress and project results in project plans, status reports, and other documentation. The second one is the warriors. These are the people who can cause the desired outcome to happen. Only 10% of the project managers are warriors, so this flavor is a rare one. They make the news rather than merely document and report the information. They are leaders first and are persistent in their quest for project milestones and completion. They dare to speak up, stand up, and confront when required. Indeed they are willing to surface issues quickly and get points the attention of the amount needed rather than letting them kill the project. They accept responsibility, demand accountability, and won't take no for an answer. They work tirelessly and effortlessly to go over, under, and around obstacles, and they form a team with having a similar mindset. They focus on the goals along with the process, neither just the process nor just the destination. Failure is not an option for warrior project managers because they find an answer and get it done. On the other hand, the bookkeeper PM would document the risk, issues, and roadblocks, prepare slides explaining why the dates or the project will be impacted. To ensure the project reached it's desired finish line, every organization needs a warrior project manager.

The bigger the project, the more critical this is, but one has to be able to recognize, hire and harness the right kind of warrior PMs and, if required, provide them with the project coordinators who can ensure the project documentation procedure is followed. If delivering a product is an art, and the developers and architects are the artists, then Project Management is an art, and all the project managers are the artist. In my opinion, Project Management is a form of art, which required a high-level leadership component. The paperwork and process should be enough to enable the project team to function in a coordinated manner and facilitate communication within and outside the project team. Anything and everything beyond this is wasted effort and is often counterproductive. I have seen leaders who demanded two years roadmap for every IT function yet had a proven track record of never delivering anything on time, on budget. In a time of high-level business change, the leaders should decline such a roadmap, and they should focus on a six-month rolling plan, with a commitment that the team would always deliver on those commitments. Leaders and their team would need fantastic perception and morale to deliver their commitments based on the six-month rolling road map and repeat the same repeatedly. The organization who follow these principles always value a thick set of plan and documentation rather than actual results. A bookkeeper is not the warriors who ruled the roost. So, recruit, build, and celebrate warriors.

Break the little glass. Failure should not be an exception, nor should it be readily accepted. Plan to win!

Ten Basic Principles of Project Management

Failure is not an option: If you are going to fail, then failing faster is much better than falling slow, as it could help you to get your showstoppers out in the open and under discussion.

The project team will kill themselves to accomplish and exceed the goal: If the project is evident on the project goal and believe that their leaders think they can do it, they can go any extra miles.

Management is over-rated, and Leadership is under-rated: Focus on Leadership! Develop and invest in a relationship at all levels in all functions impacted by the project.

Focus on the end goal: You only need a process to achieve your end goal, not the goal should align with your strategy and bureaucracy.

Figure out your critical resources and protect them from outside demand: Identifying the key or essential resources and protecting them from external demand is one of the vital aspects, and this is the area where most of the leaders surrender themselves.

Project Documentation: Project Documentation should serve the project, and it's one of the vital aspects to make every project successful. The documentation can help you to focus on your goals and the results by paying similar attention.

Opinion and Advice: Many people have opinions and advice on what should be done, but only a few can trigger that to happen, and those few are called warriors.

Accountability is everything: Distributing accountability within the team is the key. The warriors not only distribute the team's accountability, but they ensure the team takes it up positively.

Never plan a project using duration: Effort is what matters. 90% of the projects are planned using duration, which is the main reason for project failure; even though they succeed with struggle, they may not achieve the benefits of a project.

Communication: Communication is the primary skill, and it is the bread and butter of a project manager. To make the projects successful, every project manager should communicate effectively. The communication can be diplomatic and straight, depending on the situation, but it can't be bold or over-expressive at any given time.

Conclusion

Based on my professional experience, I have noticed that Project managers often ended up doing coordination work. I have seen many project managers with PMP, and other relevant certifications ended up doing the coordination work, which is a little unfair to all those project managers. Organizations need to have a clear mindset on their resource requirement; if they feel that they need someone just for coordination and administration work, then they can always recruit a project coordinator instead of project managers. Hiring a project coordinator will be a cost-saving for many organizations, and they can do the coordination and administration work without any haze. Project Managers should be thinking of themselves as what they wanted to be because both warriors and bookkeepers are the two different characters of a project manager. Here both Organization and Project managers are equally responsible for defining the character of a project manager. Only in some cases, the project manager comes out as a warrior due to their natural character, but in many cases, they are adaptive, suppress their warrior character, and become a bookkeeper.

Chapter-9

What is EPMO? and How do we differentiate both PMO & EPMO groups and manage both the groups seamlessly

What is EPMO?

An EPMO is a centralized business function that ensures a strategic alignment between your business objectives and the number of projects executed. This centralized office's primary goal is to provide organization-wide guidance, governance, standardized processes, project & portfolio management best practices, tools, and techniques. Mainly organizations with a global presence feel the impact of non-uniformity the most, mainly where technologies and processes differ regionally. In short, it's the strategic arm of decision-making that informs resources of how value is created across the enterprise.

//The purpose of setting up an EPMO is to record, analyze, and present information to senior leadership, which will enable them to see if a program roadmap is tested thoroughly. //

Introduction

The worth of Project Management Offices (PMOs) and Enterprise Project Management Offices (EPMOs) has raised many questions for many years. They have always been criticized as overhead and lacking tangible results. "The great recession time" has presented an opportunity for EPMOs to demonstrate their values.

During the period of crisis, organizations struggled financially, and funding for their project became inadequate. It has become critical for organizations to align their project investments with their strategic directions during a crisis or recession time. The importance during such time is to execute on these investments and reap their full intended values. For all these reasons, the concept of an EPMO was created. The approach utilized by is called strategy to execution.

Difference between PMO & EPMO

EPMO	PMO
EPMO is typically outside of any operational business unit and reports directly to CEO or CFO	PMO is aligned with a business unit, often within IT and reports to CIO or CTO
EPMO responsible for all programs and projects across the enterprise and creates a top-down view of an organization's portfolio of projects	PMO is responsible for all projects and programs within the business unit.
Assist executive leadership in deciding which programs and projects should be undertaken. Create a clear vision of short and long term strategies.	There is a wide variety of PMO flavours, but they mainly adopt three models. 1. Supporting PMO 2. Directing PMO 3. Controlling PMO They also operate in three levels of oversight those are: 1) Project Management Office 2) Program Management Office 3) Portfolio Management Office
EPMO required strong Accounting and Analytical skills to evaluate the return on investment for proposed projects. EPMO leadership should have steady business knowledge and comparatively less technical than business unit project managers.	PM's within PMO required to have project management technical skills and training. Usually, they should be having some level of subject matter knowledge based on their parent business unit. They also required to have strong, soft skills and skills to build good personal relationship within their group.

Here is the graphical representation of how EPMO differentiates from other PMOs

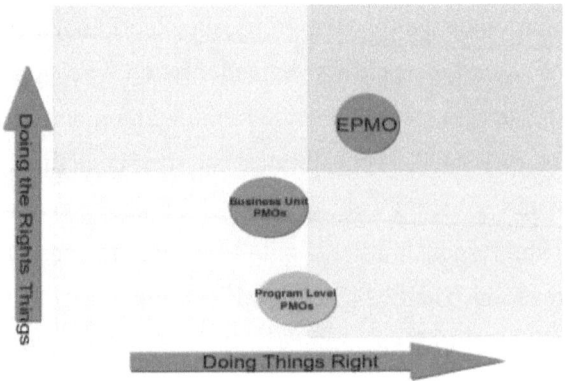

The overlap between EPMO and PMO

There are several areas of responsibilities that may fall under the EPMO or PMO, depending on the company culture, goals, tradition, and other factors. Often these responsibilities are shared between the groups. Ideally, in this case, the EPMO defines methodology, tools, metrics, and PMO is responsible for implementation. So, the below-mentioned responsibilities may overlap.

- Project Management Methodology (PPM)
- Portfolio and Program Management (PPM) tools
- Project Performance metrics
- Best Practices
- Resource Management

When can EPMO and PMO work together

EPMO and PMO can work together. If there is a distinct definition of objective for each group, they work together really well. Both should have clearly defined mission, vision, goals, objectives, success measures while limiting commonality and vagueness. Roles and responsibilities can then be defined and aligned with their team's objective. Each of these group's purposes and responsibilities should be cleared to everyone in the organization. The EPMO and PMO should work to support each other. The EPMO determines which project should be undertaken based on company strategy and project value, whereas the PMO should successfully manage and implement those projects. When a PMO is directly accountable to the business leadership it is servicing, then it becomes most useful. A dotted line reporting to the EPMO is also appropriate to ensure that the PMO is reporting the necessary status, metrics, working on the appropriate projects, and following any standard set by the EPMO.

When EPMO and PMO tend to see a conflict

Sometimes establishing EMPO and PMO within the same organization can be tricky. If these groups are not set up correctly, then there might be competition and redundancy between them. If the roles and responsibilities of EPMOs and PMOs are not aligned.

Then It may result in hindering project execution instead of helping advance company goals and objectives. Senior leaders must support both the EPMO and PMO groups equally while providing a clear delineation of responsibility between the groups. There are instances where executive leadership establishes and EMPO, and IT creates a PMO without effectively collaborating. So, in this case, both groups get confused. As to their mandates, and eventually began to compete for attention and resources. Usually, in this case of scenario, where to place the project managers can also be a point of contention. There were cases where an organization has its project managers in both the EPMO and PMO groups without properly defining their roles and responsibilities. Some organizations assigned two PMs, one from the "Business" EPMO and one from the "IT" PMO. Usually, this is the type of case or scenario where both groups tend to fail miserably.

Where EPMO and PMO succeed together

Successful EPMOs are focused on company strategy and ensure the right projects get approved. EPMO is a small team of senior, business knowable individuals and aligned closely with senior leadership. They might be responsible for establishing high-level project management best practices and perhaps tools, which typically collect the project status and metrics and report overall portfolio health to senior management. Effective EPMOs are staffed with experienced, professional project managers with subject matter knowledge.

The EPMO has mature methodologies, which aligned well with company culture and are viewed as adding value by their customer business unit. Usually, highly productive PMOs focus on the project deliverables and meeting business expectations, not on the process.

Conclusion

One Size doesn't fit all. EPMOs and PMOs should be tailored to fit within the company structure and culture. Start with your organizational goals like reducing costs, increasing the project success rate, selecting the right projects, and evaluating how best to meet these goals given your respective company culture. Some companies build their PMOs based on academics and best practices without considering their context. The best and advisable thing is to take a small towards implementing an EPMO or PMO. Try to develop a long-term vision and strategy based on your company goals. Then, develop a plan that aligns with your strategy, rollout the PMOs in phases, making adjustments to the plan based on the feedback and lessons learned. During this entire process, you are sure to have executive buy-in and over-communicate along the way. Everyone involved in this process should understand PMOs purpose, how it adds value to the organization, and why it's good for them.

Reference:
http://aprelion.com/epmo-vs-pmo/

Chapter-10

The Secrets of Successful EPMOs

Straight from Heart

We all know that "EPMO" stands for "Enterprise Project Management Office." The poor performance of projects is a blight to an enterprise. When a project misses its goals and targets, they challenge the Organization's ability and a drain on resources. Based on my experience, I have seen that many investments are wasted due to poor project performances. When Organization strives to hit its targets during uncertain times with the set of resources, which are likely to remain limited for the foreseeable future, the Organization should consider deploying EPMO, which can tune in to perform at the top of their game.

EPMO operates at a strategic level by collaborating with executives to ensure that Project and portfolio activities are directed to the overall business's benefits. Many organizations have transformed from traditional PMO structure to EPMO, and some of the new organizations have outlaid establishing EPMO right out of the gate. An EPMO offers real benefits, including higher projects, programs, portfolios, and strategic goal execution. It takes a significant amount of time and effort to build an effective and efficient EPMO.

The success mantra of an EPMO depends on some of the critical factors. I am going to explain those key criteria today in my article.

Culture and Talent Management

People and Culture are vital aspects of EPMO success. It means recruiting and training the right mix of skills and establishing team-wide resiliency and empathy becomes significant for EPMO success. In the current time, organizations emphasize leadership skills as much as they do for technical skills. The High performing EPMO focuses on their hiring practices and training programs on technical skills, Leadership Skills, business acumen, and digital skills. When it comes to leadership, the successful EPMOs focus on being empowered from the top. The execution of projects, programs, and portfolios relies heavily on how teams and functional units work together and how resilient they are during crisis or disruption. Leaders are expected to demonstrate empathy, and in my opinion, empathy is directly related to a company's financial performance.

Strategic alignment

Strategic alignment is mission-critical for an EPMO to align all the projects, programs, and portfolios activities to Organization-wide strategic objectives.

When projects are executed but don't align with organization-wide goals, then the resources, time, effort, and money we spent on the project are not fully capitalized. It could harm overall company performance. An ideal high-performing organization recognizes this situation in the early phase. They only approve the projects when they have a proper business case, which outlines benefits and how each of these benefits is tagged to the goals set out by the leadership team. When the goal changes Organization-wide, the EPMO should re-evaluate the projects and programs to ensure they are still aligned with the Organization's direction. The EPMO should not feel shy to cut the projects that no longer align with organization-wide goals.

Normalize Project Management

The EPMO should normalize project management practices to align with the Organization's high-level strategic goals. To do so, the EPMO would require careful and methodical planning. The EPMO can improve overall project efficiency, increase the chance of achieving success at every level, and decrease the risks by implementing the Project Management processes and procedures which can be adhered to across organizations. An organization must tune in their internal processes and best practices to be more innovative, efficient, and effective while managing or addressing the risks and achieving success.

Without suffering failure at some juncture, it is unlikely that the Organization can undertake additional innovative projects, but one can only juggle with a limited object with two hands. Having normalize and efficient EPMO practices can allow your Organization to allocate more of its resources and budget towards innovating and increasing its competitive advantage.

Benefits Driven Approach

Successful Organizations always identify that investment dollars must be spent wisely, and the projects must be driven towards meaningful and measurable results. EPMOs are instrumental in helping organizations to identify and achieve sustainable benefits. A project without clear goals and benefits is like driving a car without having a destination in mind. So, each potential project must be backed by a comprehensive business case that explains the project's purpose, links the same purpose to the Organization's goals, and clearly defines the benefits, which are expected to be realized upon completing the project. It should also identify the Key performance indicators (KPIs) that can measure the Project outcomes, determine whether the project is successful or not, and demonstrate how the project achieved this success.

The Learnings

Successful organizations prioritize a culture that focuses on accountability, delivering customer values, receptiveness to organizational change, investment in technology, and placing values in project management. So, by developing an EPMO culture that can focus on talent management, strategically aligned projects, normalized processes & practices, and benefits realization, which can help organizations to increase their performance and achieve a higher rate of success.

Chapter-11

Common Project Management Mistakes and how to avoid such mistakes

Introduction

We all have witnessed that some of the Projects complete seamlessly; there can be many issues, which can arise along a project's journey from ideation to sign-off. Dealing with all such problems calmly, patiently, and efficiently is crucial for a project manager's role. Some of these challenges a project manager will face can be relatively easier to handle on the fly. Others, however, will have a more significant impact on the success of the project. There are inevitable common mistakes that play a vital role in every project's success. So, we will understand each of them and their risk management strategies and advice for heading them off before they could derail the project progress.

Misaligned strategic Objectives

All the projects that an organization launches must tie back to organization-wide goals and objectives. When we have valuable resources and time to execute a project that is not aligned with the company vision, it placed the project at a higher risk and the business's long-term success.

Each project should have a strong and approved business case that spells out how it aligns with the executives' goals to ensure the misalignment of strategic objectives. Each of the project goals must be documented to ensure the project is specific, measurable, achievable, and relevant to organization-wide goals and objectives. The best option is to identify all the goals and document them in the project charter so that it creates better clarity about the project's purpose and stick to those purposes by revisiting the project charter and aligning team efforts around it.

No Project Sponsorship

The way the project team and stakeholders rely on the project manager for support and guidance, the same project managers also rely on the project sponsors for the same. A Project Sponsor is ideally a member of the executive team, and the person is treated as a Project champion as they can provide project insights and help the project managers to resolve the conflicts when escalation is necessary. Sponsors also play a vital role in setting up the right tone for the project to influence buy-in throughout the organization. Change is usually not accepted by most of the stakeholders. Without a sponsor, the project managers can be left flounder with executives, cross-functional teams, clients, and end-users. So, a Sponsor can help pave the way for the project managers. Every project should have a sponsor who initiates the conversations with executives and other leaders about why a project should go ahead.

Not only start the conversation, but they also convey the benefits, who will be assigned to lead the projects, and request the cross-functional leaders to share the information with their department.

Poor capacity planning and resource management

Before the organization can allocate and manage project resources, they need to plan the resource capacity. During the planning phase, the right set of resources required for the project need to be determined and identifying the pool of available resources. So going past this process could risk the project. Usually, many organizations use various tools to run what-if scenario planning during the planning and resource management phases. They use the what-if scenario planning as a risk management tool to test the impact of assigning, managing, and shifting project timelines and resources. So, what-if scenario planning offers many benefits. It helps an organization identify resource options in real-time, balance the workloads, and optimize the usability of all the resources to ensure that the team members and stakeholders are not being overallocated. Alongside this, the what-if scenario also ensures that the task or project start date is not negatively impacted.

Misaligned Methodologies

Project management methodologies provide a set of standards to follow to the entire project team. Choosing the right methodology to execute the project is vital to the project's fast and accurate delivery. So, executing a project without an effective methodology or aligning project and team expertise to a wrong methodology can increase the project's risk factor. There are methodologies to choose from; each of these methodologies serves a different purpose, but sometimes they also serve an overlapping purpose. Project management methodologies usually guide the project team to meet project goals and objectives. Some well-adopted methodologies are meant to reduce product defects; some ensure the project processes are effective and ensure faster delivery of products or services. So, it is significant to choose the right project management methodologies, which match the project team's capability.

Communication Breakdowns

As per the PMI research, 20-30% of the project failed due to ineffective communication. Many factors contributed to poor communication and communication breakdown in day-to-day activities and project work. Communication styles or methods, existing tensions, conflicting goals & objectives, untimely communications, and miscommunications are among the other issues which can cause severe damage to a project.

Considering communication as an essential aspect of effective project management, developing an effective communication strategy is vital for achieving project goals and objectives. Developing an effective communication strategy required a project manager to know and understand their audience and the value of each of the audience. Communication should be timely, frequent, clear, and transparent.

It is equally necessary for a project manager to sound inclusive, respectful, and consistent throughout the project, helping the projects progress smoothly.

Right Software and Tools

It is impossible to successfully deliver a project or meet the project goals and objectives without subsequent project management software and tools in place. Without having proper tools and software, it will be risker for the project manager to plan, execute, and monitor the projects and unlikely to be successful. Without having proper tools and software, even the smallest company and the smallest project will also struggle. Managing larger projects that have multiple goals, tasks, and resources can be a daunting task without having the support of the right software and tools; before contemplating which project to tackle its necessary to identify and evaluate the right project management solution which can help the team to manage tasks, resources, and schedule of work and collaboration.

Conclusion

Addressing these standard project management issues can help overcome the daunting risks and always keep the project right on track towards benefits realization. It is critical to look seriously at the topics mentioned above and take necessary steps to address them before they are late, so that project sponsors, project managers, and project teams can deliver the projects successfully and can able to derive the benefits realizations. Projects seldom go as planned, leaving project managers with any small number of flames to put out, so such common issues can be a showstopper in a project.

Chapter-12

Project Managers have all the skills to become CEO, but why they don't?

Introduction

The project managers are one of the best candidates to become CEOs because they carry out their usual work by bringing together all the different aspects of the theory, reality, vision, process, finances, value, politics, and human nature to create sustainable and successful outcomes. Project managers often manage projects which cross all organizational functions, and they visualize the organization as a whole entity rather than the soiled view of a particular functional program. When a project manager demonstrates the success of managing enterprise-level projects and organizational resources from a holistic perspective, they should be viable candidates to move up to a CEO level position. For those interested in moving up in this direction, then the CEO position should be a natural end to years of experience. However, over a period of years and decades, we all have noticed that CEOs are hardly ever come from a project/ program/ portfolio management position or background.

Resembling Career path

The CEOs usually come through a limited channel, either from within the organization or outside the organization. But they have a resemblance to the career path of a project manager.

- ***Finance:*** If the organization requires cost containment, cost reduction, and benefits realization.
- ***Sales/Marketing:*** If the organization has to increase its top line and focus on business development
- ***R&D/ IT:*** If the company is highly technologically driven
- ***Operations:*** As often, the COO (Chief operating officer) is the one running the internal side of the business, but the overall accountability lies with the CEO, and it comes as a natural move.

Skills and competency required to be an outstanding CEO

Becoming a CEO is the most significant leap that an executive can make in their career. The complexity of the role and the skill required to successfully manage this complexity make the CEO stand out in the pool of ordinary resources. Successful CEOs can deliver business results by maximizing stakeholder's value, measured in terms of economic value added (EVA) or any other metrics such as "earning per share," profits or sales, and any other business strategic goals defined when they are onboarded.

Being popular and charismatic may help them substantially because emotional intelligence facilitates leadership. Below mentioned attributes are the key differentiating factors.
Forward Thinking: Plans ahead and prepared for the future.

The ability to perform effectively in a complex and challenging environment (Intrepid): Comfortable to take the calculated risk, not careless risks, biased towards execution but not too impulsive, Actively and optimistically pursues new opportunities, Thick-skinned and persevering but not insensitive.

Team Building: Seek to understand different perspectives but should not over-analyze, Display intensity or emotions but should be able to control the same, Involves others in the decision but should also be an independent decision-maker, Comfortable with multiple arrays of personality but should not over-trust anyone.

What is so different about being a Project Manager?

A Project Manager in an organization is ideally exposed to decision-making, which is the driving force of success. Observing how the right decision is made and understanding the analysis which is undertaken to reach those decisions are essential to moving into a leadership position. Ideally, the project manager will be engaged with mostly all the facets of business in an organization, if not all (i.e., IT, Sales, Marketing, Support, Procurement, etc.).

There is a common belief that the Project managers are like the CEOs of the project; they have to answer to the steering committee and are responsible for project execution of strategic initiatives. If this is the case, then why don't more project managers become CEOs? To understand the situation better, let's look at the project management skills. According to PMI and other academic studies of project management, a project manager's qualities are categorized into the following three areas.

Project Management Core Skills: These skills include planning, managing, organizing, managing risk, anticipating issues, and coordinating work.

Technical Expertise: This gives the PM the credibility to provide leadership on a technically based project, the ability to understand essential aspects of the projects, and the ability to communicate in the language of the technicians.

Interpersonal Skills: These skills help in providing directions, communicating, guiding, motivating, assisting with problem-solving, and dealing effectively with people without having authority. A program manager will need more leadership skills, while a project portfolio manager will require more strategic thinking skills.

Ideally, a project/ program/ portfolio manager can be considered CEO material as they meet all the CEO attributes mentioned in my previous points.

What is missing?
Despite having very similar attributes, skills, and competencies, PM-only skills don't make a good CEO, but project management experience should be a "must-have" competency of many CEOs.

Conclusion
As per my recent research, more of the large corporations are including real-time project experience as must-have criteria in the career path of all their high- potential candidates for senior executive roles. Which is a good sign that it shows corporations are changing in the right direction? It will provide real-time pain and experience as a project manager to all their possible high-potential candidates for the senior executive roles and

CEO roles. With the experience, they will always open to understanding the challenge and problem of a project from a project management perspective.

Reference
I referred to the CEO's roles, responsibilities, skills, and competencies from the below-mentioned websites and written this article based on my professional experience in Project Management.
https://managementhelp.org/chiefexecutives/job-description.htm
https://www.inc.com/articles/2001/10/23549.html

Chapter-13

Spotify Scaling Agile Model

What is Spotify Model?
The Spotify model is a people-driven, autonomous framework for scaling agile. This model emphasizes the importance of culture and network. This methodology uses Squads, Tribes, Chapters, and Guilds, whereas this model's foundation is the squad, and it acts as the Scrum team.

The history behind Spotify Model
Spotify has become a popular music player and well known for providing original and limitless collections of music content. It was launched in 2008, and it has become a large company with

having 1600 employees. They owe their success to their deeply rooted agile methodologies and utilization of the Agile Scaling in their way. This method is called Spotify Tribe. Initially, the company started with scrum methodology when they have fewer employees, but when they started to grow, they thought of scaling; thus, they started utilizing agile scaling in their way. Now they have 30 agile teams that are spread across four cities in 3 different timezones. Adopting a unique Agile Scaling Method has made them achieve their goals quicker and helps them shift people's mindset.

How did Spotify Company Managed and Scaled with times?

Spotify has initially started using scrum; soon, within no time, their work and resources scope increases; thus, they began applying agile principles in the following way.

- Squads
- Tribes
- Chapter
- Guild
- Trio
- Alliance
- Chief Architect

Here is the detailed explanation of all the components mentioned above

Squads: The Basic Unit of development at Spotify in the squad. Generally, a squad is similar to the scrum team and is designed to feel like a mini-startup. There can be multiple squads in an organization, and each squad consists of 6-12 people. Each squad is dedicated to working on one specific area. All the people in a squad usually sit together, and they have all the skills and tools needed to design, develop, test, and release to production. The squad is autonomous, self-organizing, and self-managing. Each of the squad has complete freedom to choose their agile methodology. So some squad uses Scrum sprints, some use Kanban, and some use a scrum and kanban mix.

Sometimes to release early, squads apply the Most viable product (MVP) technique too.

Each squad has a long-term mission, such as building and improvising the product. All the squads always have an agile coach that helps improve their way of working. There is a product owner who defines the vision of the feature area. The Agile coach conducts retrospective and sprint planning meetings that are kept optional. Each squad has direct interactions with stakeholders and no blocking dependencies on other squads.

Most of the squads have an awesome workspace, including a desk area, a lounge area, and a personal "huddle" room. Almost all the walls are whiteboards.

The Squads are encouraged to spend 10% of their time on "hack days." People do whatever they want during hack days, typically trying out new ideas and sharing with their peers. Hack days are not only fun; they are also a great way to stay up-to-date with new tools and techniques and sometimes lead to important product innovations.

A high-level insight of a Squad:

Product owner - The squad has a dedicated product owner that prioritizes the work and takes both business value and tech aspects into consideration.

Agile coach - The squad has an agile coach that helps them identify impediments and coaches them to continuously improve their process.

Influencing work - Each squad member can influence his/her work, be an active part in planning and choose which tasks to work on. Every squad member can spend 10% of his/her time on hack days.

Easy to release - The squad can (and does!) get stuff live with minimal hassle and sync.

The process that fits the team - The squad feels ownership of their process and continuously improves it.

Mission - The squad has a mission that everyone knows and cares about, and stories on the backlog are related to the mission.

Organizational support - The squad knows where to turn to for problem-solving support, technical issues, and "soft" issues.

Squad

- "Feel like a mini-startup"
- Self-organizing
- Cross-functional
- 5-7 engineers, less than 10

Tribes: Multiple Squads that work on a related feature area make a Tribe. The Tribe can be seen as an incubator for the squad mini-startups. The tribe has a fair degree of freedom and Autonomy. A Tribe may consist of 42-150 people, but ideally, a tribe should have a maximum of 100 individuals. Each of the tribes has a lead who is responsible for creating a productive and innovative environment for the squads. The squads in a tribe are physically in the same office, and the tribe lead can be part of the squads as well. Tribes hold gatherings regularly; maybe an informal get together where they represent their work to the rest of the tribe on what they have delivered and discussed the lessons learned.

Tribe leaders pay close attention to the squad

dependencies and analyze to what extent those dependencies block or slow the squad down. Then tribe leaders discuss the ways to eliminate the problematic dependencies, especially blocking and cross-tribe dependencies.

Pictorial representation of a Tribe

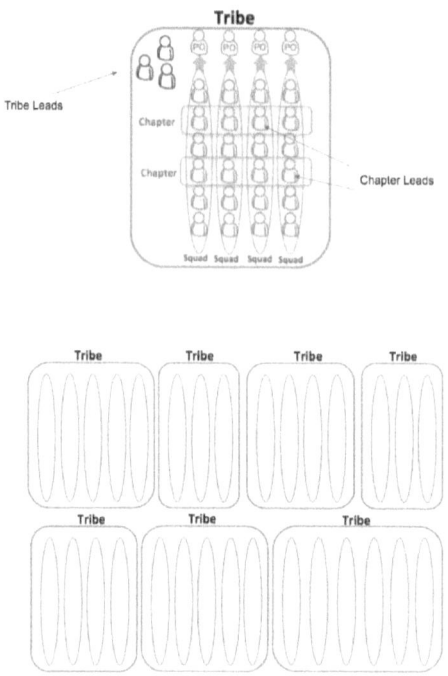

Chapter: The Chapter is a small family of people having similar skills and working within the same general competency area, within the same tribe. The chapter is a kind of glue that keeps the company together; it gives some economies of scale without sacrificing too much autonomy. A Chapter consists of individuals from different squads to be grouped into one and formed within a tribe. A Chapter lead is also a line manager of the chapter members and supports them in their personal growth and specific challenges. Each chapter meets regularly to discuss their area of expertise and their specific challenges. The Chapter Lead is also part of the squad and tribe and involves in day-to-day work. A chapter can be like the testing chapter, the backend chapter, the frontend chapter, and the web developer chapter.

Pictorial representation of a Chapter

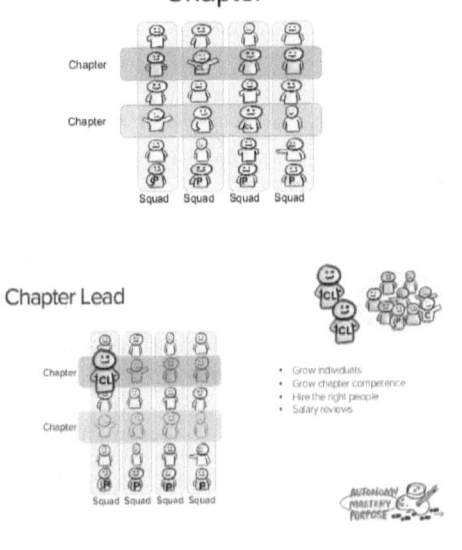

Guild: An informal group constituted of people from different tribes. A Guild is a more organic and wide-reaching "community of Interest." A guild is a group of people that share knowledge, tools, code, and practices. A Person from any squad, chapter, or tribe can be part of a guild.

The purpose of having a chapter and a guild is the same; ensuring transparency by solving problems and keeping teams aligned and focused. Simultaneously, the chapters are always local to a tribe, while a guild usually cuts across the whole organization.

A guild often includes all the chapters working in that area and their members, e.g., the Web developer guild includes all the web developers in all web developing chapters, but the benefits of having a guild are anybody who is interested can join any guild.

Now I will explain in simple terms with an example as to how a guild works. There is a tester from a particular squad, let's say from squad A, who is struggling with a problem. There is another tester in squad B who can easily solve the same problem because he has already done it, so if both of them are in the same chapter, then they can share their problem and find a solution.

But if both of them are not in the same chapter, then they would have a guild, i.e., a guild for testers, so both the testers can share their knowledge and help each other. As we have understood that each chapter meets regularly to discuss their area of expertise and discuss their challenges. But a guild usually conducts workshops, and guild workshops like hackathons and guild workshops are critical for guild members.

Pictorial representation of a Guild

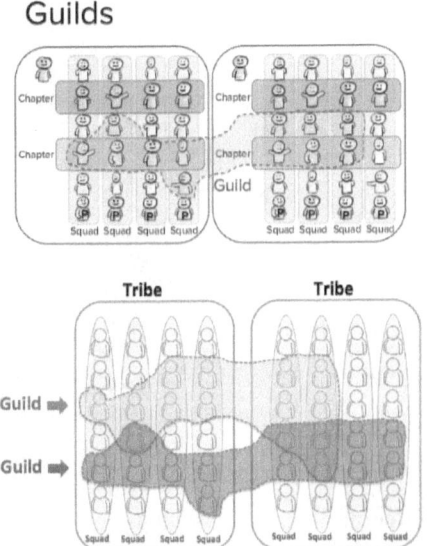

Trio/Alliance Lead: A Trio is formed when for every tribe, there is a design, product area, and tribe lead. They can also be called as Alliance lead.

Alliance: A combination of three trios makes an alliance. It is led by product, design, and a tribe leads.

Pictorial representation of a Trio & Alliance

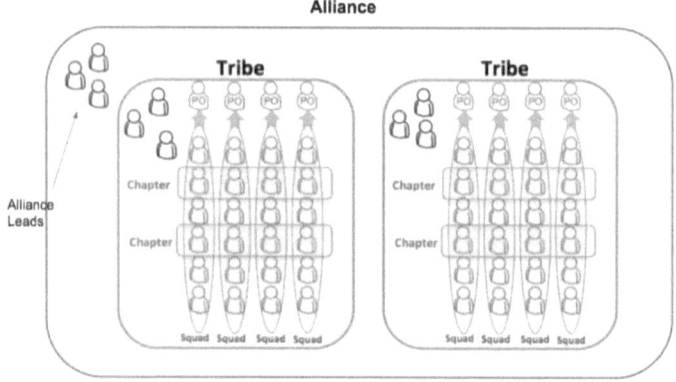

Chief Architect: A critical member of an organization that defines the architectural vision, guides in design, and deals with the system architecture dependency issues.

Distribution over Delegation: The Whole system greatly changes the company's leadership structure- especially as squads have no hierarchy. But this can be a daunting prospect for all the traditional companies as the Spotify model required to have agile coaches to help organizations set it up for. Usually, while implementing Agile, the following concerns will bound to raise, i.e., how do you ensure employees aren't slacking off? If everyone is equal, how do workers map a career path? Who is in place to delegate tasks? But we all have to remember that the adoption of agile processes increases productivity by a massive 87%. So the number itself answers everything.

If productivity increased by 87%, then it's obvious relates to the team and its members, and it happened only because when they feel motivated. They feel motivated as everyone is on a level playing field working towards a commonly defined goal. The process will also be quicker and more efficient; in return, employees will benefit from more inclusive and dynamic company culture.

SAFe v/s Spotify

The SAFe framework 4.5 is a lean-agile framework for working for several scrum teams together within the same structure. It offers a complete set of tools that range from scrum teams to portfolios. It also offers courses for its implementation and certifications to create coaches of the framework. SAFe offers a complete and detailed framework that reassures its interlocutors. But some experts see it as a framework much too detailed. SAFe tells you how to work, how to coordinate, how to train, and how to put it in place. Whether we like it or not, we must admit that it is incredibly complete. There is a small lean side to want to define everything and optimize. Overall, SAFe is a heavy framework.Spotify had set up a large-scale agile model that later became very famous in the Spotify model's name. It was Henrik Kniberg and Anders Ivarsson who communicated it in 2012. However, this model has become a reference, and many companies are inspired by it since 2012. The Spotify model doesn't want to be a big toolbox. Spotify emphasizes the need to create many interactions to limit the silo side created by the squad. It will be essential to define how each team has to work generally or leave the autonomy to the teams at 100%; usually Spotify model doesn't detail anything at this level. Moreover, the Spotify model doesn't bring any solution to manage the portfolio, unlike SAFe. Spotify provides complete freedom, and the team has to define everything. Overall, Spotify is a lightweight framework.

Conclusion

There are no losers or winners; the SAFe framework and the Spotify model both have their advantages and disadvantages. The Spotify model offers some interesting concepts that you can use. However, it will be essential to have an agile coach to help you set up. Whereas SAFe offers training and certification to understand their framework and create coaches who can guide the framework. On one side, Spotify provides complete freedom to the team to decide their way of working, and on the other side, SAFe will ask you to follow a set of recommendations for its implementation, which is much more reassuring by its strict framework side. The best option would be to use a mix of SAFe and Spotify models, and it can produce a very interesting outcome when we blend the Spotify model with SAFe tools.

Chapter-14

Digital Transformation

What is Digital Transformation?
Digital Transformation is integrating digital technologies in all areas of business. It changes the mentality of traditionally delivering the values. It improvises the operating and delivering model and the values that an organization deliver to its customer. Beyond this, it can also be a cultural change, which requires organizations to continually challenge their traditional methods.

Why Digital Transformation Matter?
An Organization may take on digital transformation for several reasons, but the most likely reason is their survival issue. Businesses do not transform by choice because it is expensive and risky. Businesses went through a transformation when they failed to evolve.

What Does Digital Transformation Framework Looks like?
Although digital transformation will vary based on the organization-specific challenges and demands, there are few common aspects of digital transformation that create a common theme or framework that all technology leaders and businesses should consider when they embark on digital transformation.

Those are:
- Customer Experience
- Operational Agility
- Culture and Leadership
- Workforce enablement
- Digital Technology Integration

While each of these elements has its varying steps, the CIO can look for the critical shared themes when developing their digital transformation strategy.

What role does culture play in Digital Transformation?

In recent times IT's role has fundamentally shifted, and CEOs want their CIOs to help generate revenue for the organizations. Earlier the top priority for CIOs was to improve the business process but now, with digital transformation comes into the picture, the CIO's top operational priority is to develop innovative new products. So rather than focusing on cost savings, IT has become the primary diver of business innovation. This shift requires everyone to rethink their roles and the impact of IT in their day - to - day experience. Though IT will play an important role in driving digital transformation strategy, the work of implementing and adapting to the massive changes goes along with digital transformation fall to everyone. So Digital Transformation is a people issue.

What drives Digital Transformation?

An important element of digital transformation is, of course, technology, but it is more about shedding outdated processes and legacy technology. The legacy technology and obsolete process hinder CIO's ability to embark on a digital transformation strategy successfully. CIO's often spend 72% of average time and budget on existing IT concerns while 28% goes to new projects or innovation. If a business wants to evolve with the rapid pace of the digital changes today, it must focus on increasing efficiency with technology wherever possible. It means adopting agile principles across business and automation of technologies will help IT organizations gain speed and momentum and reduce technical debts.

What are the key trends in Digital Transformation in 2020?

2020 will see a rapid scaling of Digital Initiatives across industries. CIOs and organizations have prepped their organizations for change in many areas but have not made the full leap of implementation in transforming their culture to embrace the change altogether.

Here are some of the key digital transformation trends that every organization, CIOs, business, and IT leaders should be aware of in 2020:

- The rapid adoption of digital operating models, including integrated cross-functional teams.

- A shakeout as those that have invested in big data governance and analytics leapfrog their competitors.
- Better use of AI and machine learning.
- Continued merger and acquisition activity in the IT outsourcing industry.
- Consultancies forming new digital partnerships.
- Expanding public cloud adoption.
- New digital transformation success metrics.
- More attention to the long-term value of digital initiatives.

How can Digital Transformation measure ROI?

To prove the digital transformation effort and values, leaders need to analyze and quantify investment return. This is easy to say but very challenging in implementing this with Projects that cross-functional and business boundaries, change how a company goes to market, and often fundamentally reshape interactions with customers and employees.

A Project such as revamping an application may have a short-term payoff, but other projects are chasing longer-term business values.

As digital transformation efforts are ongoing and evolving, which can render traditional business values calculations and financial governance approaches less effective.

At the same time, quantifying success is crucial to continue investment. Implementing the technology is not enough, but the technology must be tied explicitly to monitoring key performance indicators on customer insights and business process effectiveness. When we determine how well the digital transformation investment is performing, it's better to take a portfolio view rather than a project view. It's similar to how a mutual fund manager or a venture capital firm would look at overall performance to determine how well things are going. Digital transformation leaders must take a holistic view of digital change efforts.

This is important because the underperformance of a project doesn't reflect negatively on IT's overarching efforts. It will also help in building a tolerance limit for the necessary risks that must be undertaken to achieve real digital transformation goals. There are some of the digital transformation metrics, which every organization, CIOs, business, and technology leaders should consider.

- Set initial Metrics in advance
- Develop micro-metrics for agile experiments - The goal should be to learn and adjust.
- Incorporate business outcome: Check strategic impact like revenue growth, lifetime customer value, time to market, etc. Check operational impact like productivity improvement, Scale, operational efficiencies, etc. Finally, check the cost impact.

How to get started on Digital Transformation?

One of the most common misconceptions all the CIOs have about digital transformation is that all of their competitors are much ahead of the game than they are. That's because there is much admiration of the fastest transformer, but a little critique of how hard transformation is or how long it may take for a typical global company.

Every business formulates its digital transformation strategy, but it's smart to be learned from the CIO's and IT leaders who have already begun their journey in Digital Transformation.

Benefits of Digital Transformation

- Companies that implement a digital transformation strategy have been shown to increase performance and revenues.
- As a project manager, digital transformation helps streamline communication, improve collaboration, and shift your focus from project process and status to strategy and outcomes.
- Digital transformation allows team members to spend more time working in their creative wheelhouses, resulting in happier, more fulfilled, more productive employees.

Ways where digital transformation is changing Project Management.

More efficient and strategic communication among teams and companies: One of the most significant areas in which modern digital technology is redefining project management cross-team communication. As traditional tools like emails are cumbersome when it comes to communication and collaboration. The importance or the intent of the communication lost over endless email chains, and constant email overload tanks productivity. Whereas the collaborative work management software allows the team members and co-workers to engage, connect, and interact in real-time across departments and geographical locations. These tools cut down email clutter significantly and save loads of time in the process. These tools will not only increase the efficiency of intra-work communication; it will also improve the effectiveness as well. When team members are freed from filtering through thousands of emails a day just to keep up with project status, they can spend more time talking about the project strategy, precisely where a team should be focusing.

More collaboration within teams and ownership from team members: Along with facilitating more efficient, Strategy-Focused communication, modern work management technologies are making it easier for teams to collaborate. With the right platform in place, all the executives, project managers, and team members can add comments, assign tasks, organize dashboards, prove and approve assets, and handle everything else related to the project in one convenient solution.

More focus on results rather than process: As Digital Transformation automates the workflows and coordinates traditional project management tasks like scheduling, So PMs will get more time to focus on strategy optimization, benefits realization, and Project Delivery. According to PMI prediction, "As digital transformation continues to touch companies across every industry and verticals, thus it will portray all the project managers as strategic leaders in their organizations." With all the digital tools and automated processes, project managers are homing in on the best way to align each project with their business strategies and goals and delivering more successful outcomes in the process.

More analytics for improved PM processes, outcomes, and ROI: Digital transformation is providing PMs the analytical techniques to make data-driven decisions, break down patterns and trends, and ultimately enhance project outcomes and success rates.

This assists executives and managers in making better-informed decisions faster and easier than before. Apart from this, robust analytic reports help managers keep projects on track and tracking budget spent with real-time cost and labor analysis. These tools provide all the organization leaders and executives a precise insight into business impact and ROI on every project and help them plan their future initiatives and make critical decisions.

Reference
Referred to the below-mentioned document and video:
https://youtu.be/p-dZGlQesbM
https://youtu.be/WviLx5wiVyE

Chapter-15

Blending Project Management with Quantum Physics

The name "Quantum Physics" sounds very interesting and has profound knowledge within itself. Considering the principles of Quantum Physics, it is worth evaluating its potential in relation to Project Management, Risk Management, and Prioritization. Quantum Physics has its root in the management of uncertainty. The uncertainty is the key factor behind the deviation that can occur during project execution. It can also add a lot more value in Risk Management and Prioritization, which enforces us to reprioritize. After understanding the critical factors, the essential question to the Project Manager, Planner, and Risk management team is, "How should the catch-up plan be implemented to correct or recover the original plan?

To answer this question, one would require understanding these questions and the deeper or hidden meaning. I can clearly relate the question and their answers to some of the principles of Quantum Physics, which seem to match human perceptive schemes. Those are superposition, complementarity & Perturbation Theory.

What is Quantum Physics Superposition Principle?

The Quantum Physics superposition principle suggests that different states coexist, and the interference on the system is the definition of a system. I know this will not be easy to understand initially for anyone, so it does for me. Let me articulate it in a simple way; In human interpretation, it could be identified as the indefinite, ambiguous, or disseminative state. There are multiple and different ideas or concepts that are valid at the same time. The concretion is achieved when it is thought about. It is the result of thinking and reflection. Then from here, it follows through the process. The defined state doesn't exist, and there are different states superimposed at the same time, and then the concretion is forced once the process is intervened, which affects the state before the intervention. The origin and the consequence of an act are interacted and connected. The same principle can be emulated in human reasoning because an idea or thought is instantly modified and fed back when viewed with deep mental interventions.

Utilizing Superposition in Project Management

We have understood the superposition principle, and I am sure it would not have been clear to most of you, as it is the most complicated thing to understand in just one read. So, let me know to explain how one can apply the same principle in Project Management. After this, I am damn sure all of you at least will able to understand 80% of the principle.

Based on my understanding of the superposition principle, I have realized that it is essential to be aware of the "observer effect" because observing or prevailing invariably alters the outcome in progress for good or bad, regardless of the action previously taken to achieve a favorable result. So, which means by interfering, the planned action can become blurred. The challenge with this principle in Project Management would be to collect information from unobservable and take action by not affecting the course of the process and in front of an inevitable "observation" of a continuing process, trying to do with the minimal induced alteration. So to make it successful, one should at least know how and when to intervene.

- How to intervene is depends and can control the inevitable damage of the intervention. Intervention could consist of capturing and evaluating the course plan without even requesting or enquiring how results were achieved.
- When to intervene depends on the situation and should be handled by avoiding the induced modification due to the observer's effect and controlling the execution. It has a similarity with Scrum methodology and it's sprint process under the agile framework.

My other opinion is to make observation more frequent. It can be related to dividing the entire work packages into smaller increments to address the smaller observer effect. This Quantum principle can also come in handy in defining a continuous improvement strategy based on the Deming circle, i.e., planning, executing, evaluating, and acting. However, the discrepancy disappears if the results are assessed, and it's not still an active and ongoing process. When it comes to evaluation, we will intervene, and consequently, as per the Quantum Principle of superposition, we would alter the results without even knowing in which direction we need to modify them. So, having this principle in place, we will only evaluate the results or plan at the end of the planned production cycle, and then the appropriate corrective measures can be applied. It can also be recommended to use the observer effect during the monitor and control phase of a Project and note how it impacts these phases during the risk simulation.

Utilizing the Principles of Complementarity in Project Management

The Quantum principle of complementarity shows that the ambiguities complement each other, which means a specific behavior has different explanations, exclusive and disposable with a more detailed description. My above statement concludes that both explanations are incompatible, but they would rather cohabit or complement each other. In simple terms, every object has some complementary properties that can never be observed or measured simultaneously.

For humans to perceive the different ideas or concepts that exclude or cancel each other, they actually cohabitate and complement each other. This means multiple states and solutions exist for a particular problem or issue; even though they are incompatible with each other, we should always promote multiple possible solutions to a single expected or planned one. The leaders, managers, or the coordinators should be more careful not to restrict the possible solutions which their group can reach by giving them guidelines. If a leader is looking out for efficiency in a challenging environment, we cannot reinvent the wheel just by modifying the tires. Let it open to the team, think about it, and do the job without being affected by the leaders' guidelines.

Utilizing the Perturbation theory in Project Management

Perturbation theory is nothing but a mathematical method to determine the estimated solution to a problem by finding the exact solution to a relatively straightforward problem. The critical feature of this principle is to breakdown the problems into the solvable and perturbative parts. This Theory can be instrumental in the Project Management vertical, mainly when we have a problem at hand and doesn't have a known exact solution to the same problem, whereas we know that the same problem can be expressed as a small change to the known solvable problem.

Being a Project Manager, I have faced specific issues, where it is always challenging to find out the exact solution to the same problem. So I tried using this Theory multiple times, and it worked wonders for me. The Theory has been taken from mathematics, which can help project managers solve a problem, and then by using the existing solution, this Theory can obtain or approximate another simpler solution, and the entire process goes on till we get the simplest solution to a problem. This Theory can be used to find a better approximation; a process already defined for the same is known as "Fixed point iteration."

Conclusion

Quantum Physics is nothing, but it explains how everything works. The best description of Quantum physics is the nature of the particle, which makes up the subject and the forces with which they interact. The word "Quantum" comes from Latin, and it means "How Great" or "How Much" and physics, of course, we all know □. So, the particles' discovery is the discrete packets of energy with wave-like properties led to the branch of physics, which manages atomic and subatomic systems is what we call "Quantum Physics." Applying Quantum physics to Project Management is something exciting that I have been researching for many months now. I want to see the principles of Quantum physics and NLP applied to Project Management in real-time. Trust me; it can give better results and positive impacts.

This just a smaller piece of my research from the last few months. Soon I will share my thoughts and ideas through my coming articles on this topic and some other interesting topics, which can potentially change the entire course of Project Management and PMO.

Reference
Referred to the below-mentioned document and video:
https://en.wikipedia.org/wiki/Quantum_superposition
https://en.wikipedia.org/wiki/Perturbation_theory
https://en.wikipedia.org/wiki/Complementarity_(physics)
https://en.wikipedia.org/wiki/Fixed-point_iteration#Picard_iteration

Chapter-16

Revolutionize Project Management with AI, ML & Predictive Analytics

Introduction

Every company has its projects, which required planning, managing, and monitoring, be it any industry. We have been using a few tools to run the projects, and those tools are mainly designed for specialists. The tools don't do as much as they could to warn about potential problems. So, can Artificial intelligence-powered decision support systems, tools, and automation make the projects more successful in terms of costs and efforts? Can AI play a significant role in reducing costs and human errors? Can AI analyze the risk of a project, make things more efficient, and keep things on time and within budget? Here I have explained how Artificial Intelligence, Machine learning, and predictive analytics could affect project outcomes.

Visualizing the Risk

Managing a project takes more than just creating a plan and sticking to it. External changes and interdependencies in a project often make unpredictable outcomes.

Estimates and many forecasts are best when intuited and worst when guessed and handwaved. So, modern management techniques such as Agile and continuous delivery aim to reduce uncertainty by working incrementally, but still, it doesn't assure the delivery of the project. Portfolio management selects a blend of projects that balances risks and rewards, as it is hard to sustain and stay competitive if organizations only play it safe. So, assessing accurate risks is a tough job to achieve.

The risk is always probabilistic, and the human mind is not good at doing risk-based probability management. At least 95% of human struggle, some genius minds like Einstein and others can only do it. It further adds up the challenge when we have to combine many different probabilities. Thus we are prone to hope-based planning. We are all optimistic to some extent, which is natural, we all see the positive path ahead and could able to hope how this could work, but we don't have the guarantee or evidence to prove it, whether it will work or not. So, we hope it will go the way we are expecting it. It is where Machine learning can come in handy. It can help us predict the outcomes of a project using data that we already have, like the Planned start and end date of various phases of the project, to learn the team's completion rate and predict the likelihood of delivering the project on time. Estimates are always uncertain, so it's still better to put upper and lower bounds for how long the tasks will take.

We also need to put in some more information like the source of risk. Most of these information project teams will have, and the teams that don't have a rigorous process that can also use machine learning right away. If a team has a backlog and is not sure how to proceed, then Machine learning can help them find the right way. If the team has completed the best case and worst case analysis and work breakdown structure for the whole, machine learning can also provide more advice and suggestions. Tools that use machine learning such tools use visualizations of confidence and feasibility to analyze if the risks are going up or down over time, which can help project teams switch between. All the tools had to create the visuals because they need to connect with the fast-thinking, intuitive mind to help people see things to help them make good intuitive decisions. If a project starts getting a whole lot more red, then the lizard brain should have some fear.

The project team may still proceed with the project, but the project team must think about the right things. Using the tool that integrates Machine learning can provide some safety net here as if the project spends 20% more on this project, they have a reasonable probability of success. Thus it gives freedom to the project team to take the risk and move ahead. The algorithm and models the tools use are mostly designed for software development, but they can also be used in other industries.

These tools can provide integration with Jira, Microsoft teams, Primavera construction planning, Trello, feature roadmaps, and KPI dashboards in salesforce and power BI. These ML integrated tools can provide freedom in managing high-risk projects, and even it can be beneficial in the projects where risks are unknown.

Resource Management

Some of the AI tools enterprises are already adopting like predictive maintenance, which can make projects more reliable and efficient. The schedule and risk of unforeseen failure in the systems can throw a project out of the equation. So, Artificial Intelligence can be helpful by removing the risks in a project, be it the prediction for the project upfront or removing the risk in the execution. By using tools integrated with artificial intelligence can make projects more efficient. There is a lot of uncertainty during the current disruptive time, so how we deal with it creates a giant buffer. AI can help in many aspects, like tracking progress and performance, and it provides a broader view of the actual project management. In the case of an incremental project, where success is not always determined at the end of the project, AI can play a significant role in producing KPIs around reliability and quality. I experienced this in my 14+ years of a career that customer used to ask me, "Are we on track?", "How many deployments can we do?" and "how reliable the deployments are?"

So now, with the use of Artificial intelligence, we can produce KPI around the mentioned questions, which gives an exact result and indication to the customer. Apart from this, AI-based project management tools can also help in creating KPIs around Regression errors and product performance tracking. Using Artificial intelligence, we can automate things, which gives them the freedom to project managers to focus on other critical aspects of a project. Ideally, a large part of AI in any industry will automate the work, which is tedious, and letting humans focus on the work which machines can't do well.

Lowering monotonous and time-consuming tasks that aren't necessarily high value, but these tasks always show up in a project, and thus it ties up the project resources, AI comes in rescue here. It frees up the resources by taking up monotonous and time-consuming tasks and automate them. Thus, Robotic process automation (RPA) has a bigger chance of taking over many mundane, repetitive, and high-volume tasks from project managers, like merging data from a different system to coordinate deliveries and other logistics updating case management systems. Other than this, there are numerous other tasks like transferring data, moving it around between different systems, handling mass emails, reporting and filing and document processing, and sharing. We may have robots looking into various updates, status reports & data, and altering files based on the dates. Robots can also help in reminding if the estimates are due, and they can even send daily and hourly updates and reminders to project managers.

Predicting and experimenting

RPA could be useful for resource optimization and for effective scheduling, provided if we have the defined business rules or created data models that can be used to evaluate and report exceptions. It can be beneficial for transportation and logistics. There are many different optimizations where one can use machine learning, like cost routing to minimize fuel costs and maximize loads. If an organization is looking forward to using AI for project management, they can look for ways to experiment and improve as such practices help organizations grow towards a sustainable future. Many organizations are focusing today is only on the components within the project like resources, the progress against the resources, the health or performance of the resources. As this practice matures, then the next logical step would be a whole project, and to investigate the entire project, the organization needs to have an attitude of predicting and experimenting. To get predictions about the project, we need to capture data holistically about the project itself, feed it into a model, and then define the project's anomalies or common traits, making it successful.

Conclusion

The distinction between engineering and building software is that we dint know about the component of work. In engineering, that's a foot of intermediary or a yard of concrete, but we don't have it in software.

Laying tarmac is laying tarmac no matter where and when you are doing it, but adding a column in a database can be very different depending on what stage the project is in and who is doing it. In the current evolving time, if an organization and its internal verticals started treating Artificial intelligence, machine learning, and predictive analytics as their partner and allowing them to apply their human-level and emotional intelligence can be very helpful. They can help organizations and their various verticals to travel the distance concerning market availability.

Disclaimer: To write this article and to understand the AI, ML, Predictive Analytics, and RPA, I have read through various artifacts, blogs, articles, and checked free courses on Udemy. That's when it made me think about how we can revolutionize Project management using AI, ML, and predictive analytics; thus, I wrote this article :-).

Chapter-17

Remote Project Management

Introduction
The requirement for remote project management is the reality for most of the business today. But are those businesses ready for such transformation? Managing projects is a demanding job, and performing the project management activities remotely will add more challenges to it. In reality, it doesn't have to be. All organizations must identify possible barriers and probable solutions. The business should further analyze and document the team's readiness, processes, and technologies that can help organizations overcome their challenges in remote project management. Here are some factors which an organization can include in their evaluation.

The Business Prototype and Infrastructure
When it comes to business prototype and infrastructure, consider these following questions:

- Will the existing business model and infrastructure will fully support remote project management in the current disruption time and into the future?

- How is the organization physically structured, and does the existing hierarchy determine the necessary capabilities to effectively manage and meet the requirement of remote workers?
- Do the current infrastructure and technologies offer the required resources for remote connectivity?
- How flexible are the people, processes, and technologies, especially during a time of disruption or sudden change?

Value Driver

Several drivers may navigate a business towards remote project management. Some can be a higher-level consideration, such as overall business strategies, hiring practices, service delivery, and a change in the customer base. It's critical to differentiate between the key drivers that make sense to the overall business strategy versus the crowd and only turning to remote project management because other companies are doing it. The justification for making the switch to remote project management should not be entered into lightly. It should fit within the overall long-term business plan and be an improvement in terms of servicing stakeholder requirements.

The Right People

If organizations are considering transitioning into remote project management, having employees with the right attitude, capabilities, focus, and dedication to work in such an environment is critical.

If individuals lack motivation or individuals required a significant amount of supervision and guidance, they can't possibly add additional risk. And may not be the best move if the remote project management drivers fit with higher-level strategic objectives. Still, it may be necessary to hire an individual with the capabilities to execute projects remotely. Training of existing high potential employees can also be one of the best options. So, either of these options or maybe the combination of both can be beneficial to the company. Apart from this, organizations need to carefully and appropriately identify their existing employees' strengths and career interests, which has a critical role in working remotely. It has been noticed that few of the existing employees have more considerable skills and knowledge, which was previously overlooked.

The Necessary Tools

Now assume everything in place, the team is prepared, stakeholders are informed, and all the necessary measures are already considered for remote working. The next step would be to have the proper technology in place to empower the remote working teams. Many project portfolio management tools are compatible with laptops, mobile, and tablets, so before adding these technologies to the bucket, an organization must understand their strategic objectives, business needs, industry requirements, and project needs.

Along with this, an organization must identify how the tools/ software enable strategy, streamline processes, and improve collaboration before finalizing any of the tools/ software.

Business Process Impact

Business process impact is an area that will be impacted by the shift to remote project management. Since the remote project managers will be relying heavily on the usage of specific technologies for communication, like sharing of data, approvals, overall collaboration, and workflows will need to be rethought. So, it's become necessary to analyze and document these changes and identify how these changes will impact the business and its people. It is a vital area as many dangers creep around in the details where processes are involved. So, the organization should take their time to trace closely and document the existing and proposed processes and create a comparison of the current and proposed models and processes to know and understand the cracks that it can fall through. The organization can use failure mode and effect analysis to have a proper impact analysis; this way, organizations can reduce the risk of bypassing critical steps before they could transform into remote project management.

The Project Managers

A project manager with remote Project management experience is a need, not a mandatory requirement. Depending on the existing process, the maturity of an organization, and the experience of the employees working remotely, it may be possible to hire a Project manager with less remote work experience. Still, if an organization is less mature in its remote capabilities, it would be best to have a project manager bringing remote expertise to the table. There is no such guarantee that a seasoned project manager can always deliver in a remote environment. Other factors can create significant uncertainty if they are not addressed well in advance.

KPI's for Measuring Success

To measure the effectiveness of remote project management is critical to overall project success. Without being able to ascertain how well a remote project team works together or how the remote project team delivers, it's almost impossible to know if remote project management is working. A comparison report of the pre-remote project management model and a remote project management model makes it much easier to understand how your organization's remote project teams are actually performing. The key performance indicators (KPIs) should be used to evaluate success against the success baseline.

Conclusion

In the current disruptive time, many are talking about remote work, but timings and preparedness are the keys to success when it comes to remote work. Remote project management can be a great alternative to traditional project management for most organizations, project managers, and team members. Still, many might be thinking about how realistic this can be?

Well, there are absolute tangible advantages of having a "Remote Project Management" set up. Those are lower project costs due to technology advancements, improved work/ life balance for project team members, reduced travel time, increased efficiency, and increased ability to attract the top talents. Every advantage comes with its own limiting disadvantages, but in current disruptive times, the organizations must continue their business as usual. So, when they are considering transforming their Physical project management to remote project management, they can always factor in the point that I have mentioned above. In my next article, I will explain how remote work can work efficiently with detailed case studies and probable solutions.

Disclaimer: I have written this article based on my idea, which I had proposed in the PMOGA hackathon. I had created this possible layout and mind mapping document, and the same, I have elaborated in this article.

Chapter-18

How to make Remote Project Management Work

Introduction

Remote project management seems to be a great alternative to traditional project management for almost all the organizations during the disruptive time, but how effectively it works for organizations? Most people ask this question, "does remote project management really works? The answer, in general, is "yes." Then the next question comes to all our mind is "Does Remote Project Management works for organizations if they have top-notch virtual project team? The answer would be "not necessarily." There are advantages of establishing virtual teams for remote project management, which I had explained in my previous article. In case if missed it, here are those.

- Lower project cost due to technology advancement
- Improved work/life balances for project team members
- Increased efficiency and reduce travel time
- Enhanced the ability to attract the top talents

The Beginning

Remote Project Management has definite advantages, but every advantage comes with its own limiting disadvantages; but in current disruptive time, organizations must continue their business as usual. Several aspects can help organizations to vet if remote project management is suitable for them or not. So, the organization should be factored in and vet these aspects, which may impact their ability to successfully execute a project using virtual project management. I have listed all those several aspects that can impede remote project management and a possible solution in the next section.

Factors which may impede Remote Project Management

Productivity Degradation
The Most enthusiastic Project managers and team members can lack focus and have struggled to stay on task despite their dedication and determination.

Possible Solutions
- Build a virtual team with members who have the required technical expertise and possess an intrapreneurial outlook and approach to their work. People with intrapreneurial vision and mindset

naturally possess a passion for what they do; they are result-oriented, resourceful, dedicated, independent, innovative, and highly adaptive.

- Expect a high level of competence and personal integrity from all team members. This quality can't be optional as it drives the project team members' action throughout the project.
- Adopt exceptional organizational skills in all team members. If this is not a strong skill, additional training can be provided to improve their abilities.
- Clearly define team members' roles and duties, establish schedules, and regularly monitor their activity and deliverables' status to ensure nothing is falling through the cracks. It is one of the critical aspects of virtual teams due to obstacles like distance, travel, and possible cultural and language barrier which may exist.

Location, distance, or time zone issue
Project schedules can create a possible bottleneck when negatively impacted by the distance between team members, time changes that affect fluctuating work hours, and remote locations of work where communication is limited due to telecommunication servicing gaps.

Possible Solutions
- Establish clear policies, processes, and protocols to address the expected availability of team

members throughout the life of a project. Whenever possible, determine the suitable time and schedule with a team meeting.

All required members can attend to effectively manage the project and remove the location barrier due to time zone changes; this may be a small window of time per week but can significantly aid in monitoring progress effectively.

- Ensure all remotely located team members have the required amount of access to the necessary technology and documents to complete their work on time and have enabled them to communicate with key contacts and the project managers as needed.

Cultural and Legal Difference
In today's global commercial world, many organizations have projects that are spread across multiple geographical locations, sometimes creating cultural and legal challenges that must be factored into a project's success.

Possible Solutions
- In the initial stages, it is vital to evaluate and address any legal or regulatory issues that may exist currently or in the future. These types of problems can quickly and unnecessarily halt a project. Try to get the required local and/or international legal expertise

before proceeding with the project. It can also alleviate the risk of the project becoming an expensive sunk cost.

- Before initiating a project, research and prepare for any cultural or language barrier that can crop up throughout a project; this is an area that is highly underestimated but can create a potential risk of project failure due to misunderstandings.

Communication Barriers

The most impacted area of Remote Project Management is the problem related to communication and communication barriers. Because earlier teams were regularly meeting face-to-face, it was easy to gauge their facial expressions, body language, and tone of voice simultaneously. So, effectively and timely communication can be troubling for virtual project teams to achieve in a sudden changing environment.

Possible Solutions

- Project Managers will have to work extraordinarily hard to build trust with and among the team members. Work for forming virtual teams that feel and stay connected regularly. It would be good to talk to the peer project manager/ owner who has successfully built a virtual team to gain some insights. Also, find more about your team members, understand their psychology through MBTI personality types screening, establish a common ground, and build a more cohesive team.

- Whenever possible, set up the initial kick-off and weekly/bi-weekly meetings via video conferencing as people often feel more connected when they can see their face while talking.
- Try to use a different source of communications depending on time and information sensitive, timing difference, nature of the message, and having multiple arrays of personalities.
- Set a team-based reward that is tied to the team's performance, not based on individual performance.

Technology, Data Access & Security Issues

Having the right technology and tools available to all the remote project team members is critical in assuring to complete every project on time and within budget. A project can easily fall out of scope if team members can't be able to access the right set of data and documentation, which they need on time. Projects and organizations can be negatively impacted by security breaches that can put their client's and internal data at risk when teams are connected remotely. It is one more area that is underestimated and overlooked.

Possible Solutions

- Before project execution, ensure the appropriate PM/ other collaboration tools have identified their access rights and permissions for users, provisioned, and

- tested for all project team members.
- Ensure the laptops of remote project team members are encrypted and have the necessary security patches installed.
- Ensure the data are encrypted, and the sensitive/confidential data are accessed through organization intranet connectivity.
- Establish clear security protocols for utilizing all company information, resources, technologies, and external mobile devices.

Conclusion

Remote project management can work effectively and efficiently; however, several factors can impact a virtual project team's success, including the industry, nature of the project, complexity of a project, organizational infrastructure, communication techniques, technology, and team dynamics. To make remote project management successful, one needs to have a closer look at their organization's goals and resources. The success mainly depends on how well the issues are addressed in the initial stages appropriately and how well your resources, knowledge, and tools are leveraged to avoid all pitfalls. It may require specialized situational training, which will help improve schedule management, effectively utilizing collaborative tools, and improving communications, processes, and protocols.

Disclaimer: I have written this article based on my idea, which I had proposed in the PMOGA hackathon. I had created this possible layout and mind mapping document, and the same, I have elaborated in this article.

Chapter-19

The Hybrid Methodology the Freedom to Project Management approach

Introduction
Project managers used to use Work break down structure or WBS to manage complex projects from the mid to the late 20th century. It was the only available method by then, so all the project managers are well trained to use it. The desktop version of Microsoft Project was released in 1984, and since then, using WBS has become much more comfortable, and managers could plan and share their projects with their teams and the executive managers. Each of our desk/workspaces was filled with huge printouts of project plans from MS projects during this time.

Problem Statement
If a project manager is not familiar with WBS, then getting acquainted with the concept is simple. Before starting, they usually plan what needs to be done. Once the interim planning is done, we typically break down the big pieces or tasks into smaller pieces or subtasks. Then we further continue to do so until each of the tasks are well defined. WBS's only problem is that all the components and facts will not be known right at the

beginning.

Plus, the requirement keeps changes, the market changes, and the customer always comes up with some new requests. So in such cases, how do we do?

Allowing Agile to enter the game

It was the year 2000 when project management methodologies started revolutionizing. During the spring of 2000, 17 software developers, including Martin Folwer, Jim Highsmith, Jon Kern, Jeff Sutherland, Ken Schwaber, and Bob Martin, met in Oregon to discuss how they can speed up the development process to bring the new product to the market faster. So, out of this discussion, they have come up with the below two approaches.

- It shortens the delay of benefits to users to resolve the product-market fit and development boneyard problems.
- Getting feedback from users quickly to confirm the usefulness of new software and continue to improvise the same.

Though this meeting didn't result in the Agile methodology what we are using or we know today, but this meeting played a critical role in Agile's history. Agile project management has become the rage in the early 21st century. The waterfall was considered to be too restrictive and not able to adapt to the rapid market changes. Everybody thought the Agile method with its lean approach would solve the problem because almost all the projects would cost more and finish later than planned.

The best part of Agile is that the customer can see the result in a short time after the project has started, and it accommodates and delivers the requirements even though they are frequently changing. Due to the flexible nature of Agile, the requirement changes don't derail the project. Though Agile gives freedom, it not sustainable for the longer term. Because not all the projects are made equal, and all teams can't adjust to one method or the other. So now the question may come up how should a project manager start with a new project? As in Agile methodology, it is always hard to accurately estimate when the project will be completed. The constant changes to the requirement are the leading cause behind the project delay and cost overruns. So the question is, if the waterfall is not the right method and Agile is not like one size fits all, then what is it and what a project manager should do?

Hybrid Taking it over as a unanimous winner

So far, we have discussed and realized that both Agile and waterfall are not the ideal methodology that can fit and be accustomed to every condition and environment. So what is next, and the good news is Hybrid project management is gaining popularity and acceptance. Hybrid project management is combined with the best of Agile, and the work break-down structure creates new project management methods that can fit the majority of the projects and solve the problem of all the struggling project managers.

The hybrid Project Management method's beauty is such that it allows the team to start planning before the projects start, but it also helps the project managers divide the entire project cycle into short-term deliveries called a sprint. The hybrid methodology is the only methodology that can handle all the frequent requirement changes due to its iterative nature. At the same time, it can be able to deliver the products in multiple stages. As soon as a product reaches its maximum viable product (MVP), it can be shipped, and the development team can continue to work on future enhancements. In Hybrid, planning is done using the waterfall approach, and the execution and delivery are done using Agile methods.

Benefits of Hybrid Approach

The Hybrid approach makes the planning and project estimates close to accurate, and, at the same time, the team can react to market changes and deliver what the market demands in place of what the team has planned. But as mentioned, it is always organization leaders and project manager's discretion to zero down the methodology. It is still necessary to analyze and see which all projects can be benefited from Hybrid methodology and which all can be benefited from methodology like waterfall and Agile.

Conclusion

I want everyone to know and leverage the Hybrid Project Management Methodology, but this doesn't mean that I disallow or disapprove of Waterfall and Agile methodology. However, this article intends to educate everyone about the challenges that every Project Manager face with Waterfall and Agile methodology and how Hybrid methodology can play a significant role in addressing those challenges. I will explain in detail about the Hybrid Project Management Methodology. That article can make everyone understand how Hybrid Project Management Methodology works and how effectively we can use it. I am also working on a framework/Suitability matrix that can help an organization to identify which projects can get the maximum benefit from Agile Project Management Methodology and which ones cannot.

☐*Disclaimer: Views expressed in this article are my own. I have practical experience in delivering projects based on Hybrid Project Management methodologies and tried to cover that experience through this article, detailed elaborated experience I will be sharing in my next article.*

Chapter-20

Hybrid Project Management: The Blended Project Management Methodology

Introduction
In recent years, we have all seen a significant increase in Agile methodologies' popularity at the waterfall model's cost. Both Agile and waterfall methodologies have their strengths and weaknesses, and they are suitable for different scenarios. I have personally seen many organizations using different aspects of Agile and Waterfall. So in this article, I will ratify some of the practices and practitioners who combine both the methodologies.

Definition
Hybrid project management blends the waterfall and Agile methods to form a new project management methodology. Hybrid employs the thoroughness of work breakdown structure with Agile's speed and lean benefits for a new project management methodology that is detailed and fast. Most of the projects can be benefited by using Hybrid Methodology; only

small projects don't need Hybrid Methodology.

Guiding Principles

- The Hybrid Project is managed by a project manager using a work break structure with overall ownership & responsibility.
- A Scrum master supports the project manager by executing each of the Sprint.
- Continuous team collaboration is required for ongoing project reporting, analysis, and management review.

Roles & Responsibility

- Hybrid is independent of management structure, and it doesn't require a formal project management office (PMO). If some organization follows a Hybrid methodology and has its PMO function, it adds another layer of bureaucracy, and potentially it can cause delay and incur additional costs to the project, which is ideally not compatible with Agile.
- The Project manager Plays the role of a Product Manager. In Hybrid Project Management, there is either a Project Manager or a Product Manager; either is considered the project owner.
- The Project Manager and the Scrum master share direct responsibility for different divisions of the project.
- The Project Manager has overall project responsibility and ownership of the project.

- The Project Manager is primarily responsible for the front end of the project flow like Product Requirements, Customer Feedback, Components definition, and Work Breakdown Structure.
- The Scrum masters are responsible for the backend of the project flow like backlogs, sprints, and releases.
- Project Managers can create a team of scrum masters and other management staff if required.
- Each Scrum masters build their team based on the project requirements and timeline.

Hybrid Project Flow

I have given a systematic approach to the Hybrid Project Management flow in the below diagram.

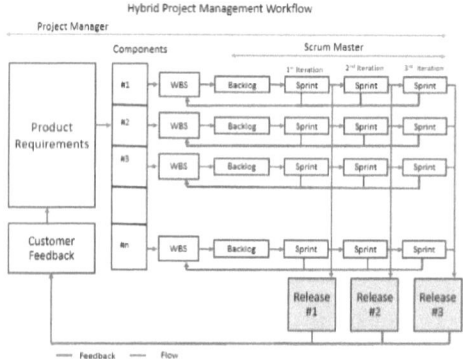

Definitions

Components: The product requirement document usually drives the modules. For example, a website has multiple components like the PDP page, cart page, shop page, account page, checkout page, and landing page. A software product will have UI, business logic, backend platform-related code changes, and communication components. So the product requirement establishes which components are required in the project.

Track: Track is the path for the development and release of each component. Track duration can vary, and not all the track duration needs always to be constant.

Backlogs: Backlog is the list of tracks for each component. The task for each Sprint is derived from the backlog of the same track. Both Project managers and Scrum masters add or modify the backlog when it is required.

Sprint: Sprint is usually spread across 4-8 weeks, and each Sprint includes development, testing, and release (deployment). Each track has it's own backlog and Sprints. Sprints from multiple tracks can run in parallel. The output from each Sprint of different tracks may or may not combine with Sprints from other tracks to make it a release.

Project Team: Each project team is made up of a certain number of team members. The essential members are 100% assigned to the project, and there is no sharing of resources across multiple projects. And team member reports their day to day activity to the Scrum master.

Hybrid Planning Phase

Ideally, in the waterfall, the entire project is scoped and planned before the project starts. But in Agile, only the first Sprint is planned. If we come to the Hybrid Project Management methodology, then the complete project plan is defined, but each Sprint's specific details are not defined until the first Sprint is completed. The Project manager owns the overall planning responsibility, and the scrum master manages each Sprint.

Project Task	Definition	Responsibility	
		Project Manager	Scrum Master
Goal	The Project Manager defines project goals for a given timeframe. There is an overall goal set, and then there is a subset of goals like product features. The delivery date for such features is set in advance.	●	○
Scope	Once the goals are defined, the tasks must develop the user-stories to develop specific features and functionalities. The Project Manager has overall ownership of this phase, and the Scrum-masters provide the detail on how each of the sprints will be implemented.	●	○
Estimation	There is a joint responsibility between the project manager and the scrum master to break down the project phases into tasks and determine how long it will take for each phase to complete.	●	●
Scheduling	With the time estimates provided by each Scrum Master, the project Manager creates an overall schedule. There are dependencies between tracks in many projects, and mainly, in this case, project managers and scrum masters work together to build the overall schedule.	●	●
Dev Start	When the development usually starts for a project, the scrum master owns the Sprint duration, and a sprint usually covers Start, Test, Finish, and Review	○	●
Review	The Project Manager is responsible for reviewing the results of the Sprint. If anything is required to be changed/modified in the next Sprint, it is usually taken care of by the Scrum Master.	●	○

● = Primary Role ○ = Supporting Role

Hybrid Process

Hybrid follows the agile methodology. Customer feedback is required at each of the iterations, testing happens and fixes to enable continuous improvement. The below-mentioned formal method can be used to define the outcome of each of the iteration.

Project Task	Definition	Responsibility	
		Project Manager	Scrum Master
Quality Control	Quality improves with design, analysis, and testing with each iteration. Quality control is based on detecting and fixing defects that occur at each iteration.	Supporting	Primary
Continuous Improvement	Lessons learned from each iteration are always applied to the next Sprint.	Primary	Primary
Project Risk	The risk was detected and resolved at each iteration.	Primary	Primary
Project Analysis	After each iteration, the overall validity of the project and its procedures are analyzed. To ensure they are inline.	Primary	Primary
Customer Feedback	Customer feedback is solicited after the release of each iteration and can modify plans for next or upcoming iterations.	Primary	Primary

● = Primary Role ◐ = Supporting Role

Hybrid Execution

In Hybrid, the project manager is assigned as an overall project owner, and the individual scrum master is responsible for executing the Sprint. At the same time, reporting is a joint responsibility that requires continuous collaboration and communication.

Project Task	Definition	Responsibility	
		Project Manager	Scrum Master
Ownership	The Project Manager owns the entire project, and individual Scrum masters own each iteration.	●	●
Task Assignment	The project manager develops the work break down structure with the help of Scrum Masters and Scrum Master perform task assignment for each Sprint. Both Project Manager and Scrum Masters manage project backlog.	●	●
Status Meeting	The Project Manager initiates and leads the weekly project meeting to review the overall project status, and the Scrum Master manages the daily stand-up meeting.	●	●
Status Reporting	The Scrum Master owns the daily status reporting, and the Project Manager owns the weekly status reporting to the management.	●	●
Quality Assurance	Daily testing activity dedicated by the Q&A team and developers for any issues fixes. Regression testing is conducted before each version release.	●	●

● = Primary Role   ● = Supporting Role

Tools Enabling for Hybrid Project Management methodology

Hybrid Project Management is always supported by method and proficiency that include the followings:

- **WBS:** to define Work Breakdown Structure, one can use Gantt Chart, Subtasks, milestones, and dependencies to define a project altogether.
- **Agile:** Kanban Board, which can show each task's position during the project development cycle.

- ***Collaboration:*** Collaboration can be in the form of real-time status notification and updates for the entire team, and integrating the details like WBS, real-time status, project progress into the project plan for providing the project visibility to management can come in handy.

Conclusion

My previous article talks about how Hybrid Project Management methodology can provide freedom to the PMO and project management methodology. So in this article, I tried to explain various aspects of Hybrid Project Management. I tried to explain those aspects, which could raise a question in anyone's mind, like definition, guiding principle, process flow, roles & responsibility, Hybrid planning, process and execution model in detail, and the tools we can use Hybrid Project Management methodology. Tools part and probable Q&A I will cover it in a separate article that can draw a holistic picture, and pre-emptively help answer all the questions. But I believe this article can help all of them looking out for some detailed level article or document to refer specifically for Hybrid Project Management Methodology.

Disclaimer: Views expressed in this article are my own. I have practical experience in delivering projects based on Hybrid Project Management methodologies, and thus I can detail out through this article. I did some background research to ensure my knowledge is in line and cover the gaps from an author's perspective.

Chapter-21

What does P Stand for in PMO?

Straight from heart

When I ask the question to my peers and friends that what does P stands for in PMO, I always got a typical response like "Projects," "Program," or "Portfolio." How about "Power," "Potential," and "Pioneer"? Why I am referring to these three, let me explain. Processes and governance are vital aspects to ensure smoother Project execution and delivery, but to ensure the successful outcome and make it happen, strong leadership skills are essential. The next question would be to what extent leadership skills are critical? The answer is straightforward; the most significant project outcome is mostly down to the leadership skills and the project team's capabilities running the show. I have witnessed this in my career, and I, too, believe this wholeheartedly. Now one may ask, then how about the worst project outcomes? For the worst project outcomes, I always use a single word, "team," and use such words intentionally. Because I believe it's not down to the Project manager or the portfolio manager or maybe the head of the PMO for that matter. I think it's a team effort, and we all know that a successful team will have great leaders.

Thus the strong leadership skills have become essential for making a project successful as they can differentiate success and failure.

Creating the Difference

If someone is looking to improve their PMO or looking to advance their career as a Project Manager, they need to pay strong attention to building strong leadership skills. As per my experience, Project Management Offices led by strong leaders can achieve better results and outcomes. The individuals who have equipped themselves with Strong leadership skills can earn the currency they needed to climb the management ladder.

Second best Job in the World

As a Project Management professional, I always think that I have the second-best Job in the World. I still believe that I have the best Job until my multi-talented wife showed me otherwise. Though what we do is excellent from CIO to Project Managers and the Project Team, we are the change catalyst within our organization. Our Organization's IT strategy and the entire business strategy is effectively a Project Manager's responsibility. It is the vision, clarity, Communication, and thought of a Project Manager, which turns the hazy conceptualize projects into a significant market disruptor. Personally, the Project Management/ Project Manager role is exciting, and it's never meant for the fainthearted, timid, or Reticent nature of individuals.

It's not only a role; it's a heck of responsibilities and takes the real strength of character. So it's not a role or a most sought job, but it's something that can define & refine one's character.

My Research

I have been doing much research on the "importance of Strong leadership in Project Management." I did search this on google, and it throws me 10+ million results. Well, practically, someone cannot go through all ten million-plus details. So, I checked some of the posts and articles, and most of them appear to be a list of attributes that strong IT leaders must-have. It also shows some books, videos that can turn someone into a great leader. The lists are worth a browse, though they are mostly listed a few of the obvious things like "Clear Communicator," "great motivator," "controlling your emotions," but apart from these, those are a good read for anyone. But one thing I observed that all those articles or posts are missing one of the critical elements. Great leaders indeed need to have "integrity" & "delegation" skills, and they also need to be a "great team builder." Still, I believe it's only 20% because the remaining 80% is always either, You, me, we, or us, i.e., the CIO, the Project Manager, and the Project team. Apart from all, it's an individual's USP, DNA*, and culture, which makes you a great or a strong leader.

Difference Between Success & Failure

The difference between success and failure is always you, me, we, or us. Technically there is no book, article, or post that can ever make you a great leader. The mistakes that we made, the lessons that we learn from our mistakes, and our success teach us to become a great leader. Overall it's a career-long process, and the leaders never stop learning. It's a journey that a person has to travel through with having lots of exciting ups and downs. I have added an asterisked DNA because it's a question that has been raised for ages that "Are the Leaders born or made?" Well, it's a mix of both. I have personally seen some people are born leaders. They started good, got very good and now they are excellent. If I had to put a number or percentage for born leaders, it would only be 5-10%. Some have given it a go, no matter how hard they try, how many books they read, or how many seminars attend, but due to their nature, they will never make it to the league of the great leaders. If I had to put a number for these categories, it would be 10-15%. I never meant that these people are not so important, but the novice may not represent the epitome of teamwork and leadership. It only serves as an exciting demonstration of multiple roles when needed to achieve or not to achieve a particular task. They are still essential for smoother project execution and delivery, and they become a crucial part of the successful outcome, but they are not the actual leaders.

The CIOs have Project Managers, who are not genuine leaders but can buy in "strength" like a commodity by accessing the Project Management as a service market. Here are the attributes of strong leadership like robust vendor governance, effective SLAs, and KPIs that can be bought in from Project Management service partners who can make it look good and sometimes even better.

Creating the leaders

There is a large space between the two groups of "high-flyers" and "buy-it-inners," where most of the rest of us carry out our trade. Between 75% t0 85% of very good or great, strong Project Leaders were not born, but they are made. I mean, they always have the spark, untapped potential, which inspired themselves and others around them. But they are being made on a day to day, Project to Project to Project basis. CIOs' responsibilities are to nurture their Project Manager's potential and help them or groom them to become strong leaders. They are the future. Jumping out of the comfort zone is what excites me. Because 80% of the Project Leaders are not born, taught in a book, or read in an online list, they are made. It's only because of you, me, we & us. Whether you are a CIO, a Project Manager, or a Project team member, you are powerful as you give birth to a future leader. If the market for this approach is around 80%, then the potential is huge.

What makes a leader be a Strong Leader?

Based on my experience and observation so far, one can become a strong leader only by "knowing themselves." I have worked with various Project Managers, and only a few of them are self-aware and know themselves well. The rest of the Project Manager's don't seem to be looking entirely into the mirror of themselves. The reason why I am emphasizing the point" knowing oneself/ Themselves" is because if someone is not able to see their faults or not able to see their mistakes, then how will they know where to improve? You can make Chicken dumplings from fish, no matter how hard you try or how religiously you follow the recipe. You will end up with Fish dumplings. Some Project Managers' careers are built on a false foundation because they can't see that from where they are starting.

Culture can make you or break you.

Organization owners need to create a culture that allows honesty and transparency, where mistakes and faults are not punished or penalized. Still, it provides an opportunity to learn from such mistakes and faults. When an organization owner does it, then it encourages immediate acknowledgment and effective correction of such errors. Thus it provides a truthful mirror to the Project Manager, where they get to know themselves well than before.

The best way for a Project manager to know themselves is by inviting and, more importantly, listening to the feedback from up and down the command chain. The C-Suite executives usually provide valuable clues in their every single response. I always like to listen, and I always encourage listening objectively, not adding any filter to our perceptions. Don't project your home movie onto the feedback you are being given.

The Beginning

The main strength of a leader becomes clearer through self-awareness. When one realizes that they have fish, not chicken, you start to know and learn what to do with it. So, when you know who you are, what you are capable of achieving when you see yourself where you went, how you can improve, and when you listen without prejudice, that's when you become a more generous and stronger leader, as I have mentioned earlier that it's a career-long process. You won't be as great or as strong today as you will be in the future, but you already knew that with self-awareness.

***Now, I think you will agree with me that "P" in "PMO" stands for "Power," "Potential," and "Pioneer." If you are still not sure, please join "PMO officers" & "Women PowerUP Network," where the other prominent leaders and I groom an ordinary candidate to become an extraordinary leader. Please tune to our Podcast channel We_Relearn (https://anchor.fm/abhishek-mishra06) on 16th Nov 2020 for more such exciting topics. ***

Chapter-22

How to Cook up a Meal out of Project Management

Straight Talk

As a Project Manager, I always feel that I am the loneliest of the place, who is up late at night sweating over a project that is running late, working over the weekends, when the rest are enjoying with their friends family. I always feel I am the only person on the planet earth who has been dumped with all the challenges. I am sure each of you also had a similar feeling. The problem I am trying to solve may be the unique one for my project but take small consolation from the fact that a PM is burning the midnight oil over their own somewhere else. I have learned a lot on my own and always through my work, and so far, my learning had helped the organizations score greater IT Project success. Project challenges can be project unique, but the same approach can often be successfully applied across the spectrum of seemingly very diverse challenges. Suddenly I realized that I am not alone the way I was thinking. In fact, I have begun to learn many project management lessons from the various areas of my life.

Life Examples

I love cooking, and I prefer to cook new dishes when I get some free time. While cooking, I learned that be it a Chef, waiter, or a restaurant manager; they too deal with the challenges similar to a Project Manager at every table, every day. Now Imagine a restaurant where they are having staff shortage, their service is not so excellent, now you can imagine how the waiters would be biting their lips and trying not to convey their sense of frustration to their customers. I have also experienced this many times in multiple restaurants. Usually, in this challenging situation, one could clearly hear the crashing pots and pans and the burning smell coming out of the kitchen. The problem was compounded by the restaurant; on top of that; they are short-staffed in the kitchen. In the current situation, one could imagine the quality of the food. On top of that, a customer had to wait for a longer time for their food.

In this case, what did the entire restaurant team would do? They can apologize and can either offer complimentary food or drink. They did this to one of their customers, now what about other customers? I witnessed this during my visit to one of the restaurants 2019 summer. The table behind me was also not impressed with the service, and they had a lot more complaints than I had. They also had a child, and they waited for 45 minutes just for the soup!

Whereas they received no apology, they were offered sauces when their main course arrived too. They weren't provided a steak knife! When they complain about all these, they were only offered a complimentary sweet dish.

Result: A disgruntled customer who probably won't come back again to the same restaurant and, in fact, he may take it to the social media and other platforms, where they can review about the restaurant. I also had a similar experience- delay in getting food nearly to 40 minutes, and the taste of the food was not that great even. The restaurant offered me a free drink and was totally transparent, apologized, and accepted that there were errors in their system. They also surprised me by waiving off my entire bill as I refused to take the free complimentary drink. The restaurant manager told me that, "Sir, this is our problem, and in my opinion, these problems and mistakes are not acceptable, so there is no charge for you." When I double-checked, they confirmed, Yes! No Charge!

Result: Happy Customer

Now let me share as a project Manager what I learned from these experiences? After observing the restaurant case, here are my key learnings or take away:

Consistency: We have discussed two different live examples, which happened on the same night, parallel to one another but the customer experience was different in both cases. Each table should be given appropriate time and effort. In the instance of a project, priority should be given to the project with strategic values, and deadlines must be considered for the same. In the restaurant case, both the tables (Projects) hold equal importance, so both should have been treated equally.

Communication: Proactive and upfront communication is the key; the restaurant was upfront about their delays. When project hit issues/ risk, the PMs who communicate with the stakeholders about the delay and how the delay will be mitigated to find that they cut more slack in the future. The truth lands a person in lesser trouble than lies and cover-ups.

Transparency: The Restaurant was not only upfront on their delays, but they were also even quick to take the responsibility and "put their money where their mouth is" by defending their words and insisting on no charge for our meals. The situation was transparently communicated throughout my experience, whereas it was not the same experience for our fellow table members.

Planning: In IT projects, you have to have the right skill set and the right staff to cater to your customer needs. Failure to do so will risk your project and jeopardize your project's entire mission/ objective, whether it's dinning up haute cuisine or integrating cutting-edge IT into the legacy system. In Project management, every skill and the process itself can be bought in as a service, when "Chef as a Service" is the only thing.

Control: During my meal at the restaurant, I never ever felt that the entire restaurant staffs were entirely in control of the situation at any point, that is, till the manager waives off the charge. Without having full control, one cant has assurance on the project's success. Milestones need to be adequately mapped and kicked off so that it ensures the project success, doesn't matter you are running a complex IT project or trying to ensure your meat and vegetables are ready at the same time.

Task Management: Control is only achieved by creating a task list, delegating the tasks to appropriate individuals, and tracking their progress. Staying on top of your To-Do list either comes naturally, or one has to develop the strategies to help. The restaurant was not in control of their task list, and as a result, it cost them their hard-earned money by waiving off my meal charge.

Process: When you deliver one project, you must have a process that automatically offers subsequent training and support. Taking restaurant example, they deliver a steak; then, as part of the process, they should have offered a knife to our fellow table members, which they don't. It shows that they either don't have a proper process or may not be following the right process. When we deliver a new system, then automatically we offer training and support for the new system to keep running it.

Negotiation: Taking the restaurant example, it was evident that, when the complimentary offer was refused, then the staff weren't sure what to do next. They were so sure that their offer of free drink would be accepted, and all would be well, so the reason they don't have a plan-b. It is often undervalued and overlooked project management skills that the best PMs have in abundance.

Leadership: The difference between a Leader and a Manager becomes apparent, be it in the heat of a busy kitchen or a Key IT project. Because Managers are always following the roles and restrict themselves within a specific boundary, whereas Leaders are like blooming sunlight which can even shine in the dark cloudy sky, the Project Managers who enhance their leadership skills find their motivational and communicational skills develop spontaneously.

Critical Thinking: It is essential for making a good decision. Considering the pros and cons of different situations before selecting the best way forward is a great sign, and it's a sign of a spontaneous leader. It is what distinguishes the habitual firefighters and the Project Managers who stand out at managing issues or risks. Critical thinking is like a muscle, so the more you exercise, the more it becomes stronger, natural, and effective. The restaurant weighed up the pros and cons of waiving my bill but failed to act similarly for the fellow table mate.

Quality Control: Starting from stakeholders, sponsors, project team, and PMs, they all need is quality deliverables. When it comes to the restaurant, the word "compliment to the Chef" plays a vital role. As a result of this, a huge tip will be left on the table. In IT Project, it is on-time delivery, budget completion, and end-user satisfaction. As part of the quality control process, the IT project has stage gates or phase gates, ensuring that the project is delivered with best in class quality. Now, most of the Project Managers & organizations are prioritizing quality management as a core skill.

Retaining a sense of humor: Retaining a sense of humor can disperse the tense situation. It's evident that not all the time Project can go right, sometimes it can go wrong. Similarly, sometimes meals can be messed up.

It is okay when things go wrong in both cases, but to lighten up the situation, it is necessary to retain a sense of humor. Taking the restaurant example, I tried to lighten the situation, which went over the flustered waiter's heads who was serving me that night. They should have laughed about it or at least should have laughed when a customer tried to lighten the situation because no one died as my meal took 40 minutes. Similarly, we don't display our clients and project sponsor that we find humor in project delays. Judging by the crashing of pots and pans, the restaurant staff weren't laughing at the ridiculousness of their quandary behind the closed doors. Sometimes, laughing at the matter can be like releasing the pressure valve, and everyone can be more effective afterward.

Learning Continues

The last thing I learn from my meal is being a Project Manager, I am not alone. Everyone has their share of struggles. After the fateful meal, I observed that people in every other profession are tussling with Project Management challenges. The Airport manager always tries to keep a commuter service on time even in terrible weather, the professor trying to get the best out of the class while meeting the demands of paperwork, similarly, a doctor trying to attend a ward full of the patient against the backdrop of health authority spending cuts.

All of a sudden, I realized that the whole world is, in some way, a Project Manager. It is just that only some do exceptionally well. This is what I learned, and on a lighter note, I have learned that to get a free meal go to an understaffed restaurant on a busy day. To match my article title, to cook up a free meal, delegate the cooking task to an understaffed restaurant, and yes, it's apparent that one has to be skillful to do so! Bon Appetit!

Disclaimer: Views expressed in this article are my own. I have shared my professional experience and learnings through this article. This article is based on my observation and perspective. The real Project Management attributes and aspects I prefer to learn from life experiences, the same I tried to express through my article.

Chapter-23

The Identity Crisis of the PMO in the age of Digital and Agile Trends

The Story Behind the Crisis

The Project Management Office (PMO) role is always to assist the Project Managers with organizational methodologies, practices, and tools. Most of the PMOs also acted as Portfolio Management offices, and at a minimum, they committed to deliver high levels of data quality for leadership/ management reporting. The data typically covers the KPIs, financial forecasting, resources demand v/s capacity, top risks, and key deliverables, and there are many such data that PMO shares with the management/ leadership group. Most of the PMOs have their share of struggle when it comes to an operational point of view with identifying the tasks to plan and execute. Apart from this, PMO is always forced to justify themselves to the organization. Simultaneously they continue to provide a useful service for both short- and long-term strategic objectives and goals. For most of the organizations, the solution is to provide a catalog of services that the PMO can offer to its customers, Project Managers, and Project Management.

A PPM/ PMO tool can be purchased and implemented to digitalize the processes, produce the data, and ensure that the governance is enforced and followed stringently. Regardless Of the challenges in establishing a functional and value-generating PMO, only a few can succeed, and others ended up becoming strategy execution office. We see mostly in every organization today as more of a strategy execution office than an actual value generating PMO.

The Identity Crisis

Why am I calling it a distinctiveness predicament? The explanation is simple and can be found in the trends of recent times, where the world is more inclined towards the implementation or improvisation of business agility. In this case, every organization's top management focus always lies on "Digital Transformation." It could impact PMOs as well as the way they function and the organizational structure. The impact before, during, and after the digital transformation is the organizational implementation of agile practices and principles, in other words building a new work culture. In my experience, all such implementation or transformation not only required for an organization to understand their existing work culture and the problem statement associated with their current work culture but also it required every organization to understand the difference between Agile, Traditional, Scaled Agile, DevOps, and Digital Transformation/ Agility.

The organization must ask himself why it is really needed, and they also need to figure out the appropriate methods, processes, and system support. Otherwise, the repercussion could be very impactful because, with no time, the "Inexperienced Agile" leadership team can feel that they lost control of their business, especially in those business units which have been mostly following Agile.

If this is not addressed beforehand, we can suddenly see the PMO in the uncertainty of their own purpose. Let me explain why; as we all know and keep saying, the "P" in the "PMO" stands for "Project," "Portfolio," "Program," or perhaps "Product" in this case; there are clear chances that "PMO" will lose their identity because these questions keep buzzing me when I am thinking of this topic, those are

- How are we going to satisfy the top management demands for business insights?
- Can we convert story points to hours?
- Can we ask an Agile for a timesheet?
- Can we compare a portfolio epic to a business case?
- How are we going to simulate the scenarios across Agile and Non-Agile business units?

The question of what is mainly coming out here is whether an organization needs a PMO on top of its Agile activities?

If the answer is "Yes," then "P" in "PMO" stands here as "Power," "Potential," "Pioneer," and in few cases, "Portfolio." Portfolio because there are high chances that PMO needs to cover the diverse set of work which will cover products, projects, and initiatives. However, a portfolio management office can also find themselves in a grey zone when they cannot figure out what story and status they have to provide their management, whereas the concerns and focus remain the same for the management group.

The Main Cause

PMO mainly manages quality reviews, minimizes risks, controls the budgets, and measures progress towards milestones and deliverables. But in an Agile environment, "Story Points" and "Business Epics" won't help them much; soon, the very loved and classic question crops up "when it will be done" & "How much it's going to cost." Another thought is that many organizations are still following the same old method of doing their effort and budget estimation per hour when it comes to availing PMO services despite the business agility. Many organizations find that the capital and operational expenses are still required to be tracked because it provides them with input for their financial statement and quarterly briefing. So again, it clearly shows that we are back to the same old Traditional age of work management practice to provide accurate insights.

Possible Solution

Many of you might be thinking about what possible solution we have to address the Identity crisis of the PMO in the Agile and Digitization Age. The answer is straightforward; I believe it should come straight away from training top management in Agile's persistence and benefit, Traditional and DevOps practices followed by an open dialogue on the need for control. I, too, believe that the real PMO is a "Both-and" office. Let me put it across differently, "PMO" is a function that takes care of the sum of all work, not just the operations. Apart from this, PMO should ensure that a common language and business understandings are applied across all Agile and Non-Agile business units and workers. Elements like time, money, and resources can be comparable for all types of work and the work that can create business values from such executions; both should be aligned with organizational strategy and priorities.

Breaking the Stereotypes

In the Age of Agile and Digitization, one thing is sure that there is no single recipe for PMO what it used to be before. It's all related to organizational culture, traditions, and circumstances because some organization needs multiple PMOs based on their culture, tradition, and circumstances, whereas other organizations continue with one PMO.

However, all the organizations they have one thing in common that is the demand for overview and insights anchored in real data and at the right point at the right time. In some organizations, the PMOs are accountable for the execution of strategy and to review if the past work could able to deliver the expected benefits or not. All the large organizations usually implement "Enterprise PMO" (EPMO) as these EPMO can translate strategy to execution so that the organization can measure progress continuously and seamlessly. It's great fun to implement and EPMO.

Shifting our Mindset

As per my experience, I could able to find a common language to be used in both the Agile and Non-Agile business units more easily, seamlessly, and I am most successful in doing so. The reason because I always believe that the functions do not necessarily help the Project Managers, Product Owners, and the Scrum Masters to do better, but they ensure that the execution of all the key initiatives is always to serve the internal and external stakeholders to have a better experience with maintaining transparency. As per my opinion, the PMO Journey should always start by understanding the problem statement, issues, and challenges that they have and what they can bring to the table. The PMO can also ensure long-term organizational sponsorship and establish a straightforward service offering for its customers.

These few aspects can help the organization in making the decisions around methodologies, execution of work, and the digital support from the It systems.

Disclaimer: Views expressed in this article are my own. I have articulated this article based on my experience and observations. Based on my experience, I have observed that the objective and intention of having PMO function always lost w.r.t be remained competitive. So, PMO ended up becoming a strategy executing office rather than creating values for the organization, which shifts the leaders' mindset. As a result, PMO loses its whole identity.

Chapter-24

How did I transform myself into a better Project Manager?

I was listening to some good old music some years back, and that's when Michael Jackson's "Man in the Mirror" caught me, and since the time I hear this song, I can't stop myself thinking what a great Project Manager he would have made! The song is all about clear messages, which means communicating one's intention & vision and getting it right when you have a deadline in mind. But "if someone wanted to make the world a better place, then they should look at themselves and then make the change!" ultimately, this song made me look at myself, and I love the second bit where it says, "look at yourself and make the change!".

I am sure it won't go well down with all the Project Management experts and the writers, but the fact is often as a Project Leader, a little self-driven, and self-improvement can help you succeed in the way, which hour-long of management training and on-line courses can only dream of. At some point in our career, we understand that what we need to focus on? What we will read in those textbooks, and what the speaker usually preaches in the webinars.

By attending these webinars and reading various artifacts, we can only help us for a few days. Let me put it across this way- we usually take our notes, go back and do things differently in our Project for a day or two, and then after that, we will slip back to our same old habits when the Project gets hard. I am not sure about all of you, but this has happened to me many times.

I have been speculating why this happened to me every time. After hearing the song, I realized why and let me put that across in a simple and understandable way. In our projects, we deal with change requests, and if the case for the change is not clearly defined, communicated, and adopted by all parties, it will lower the success rate for the same change request and sink in deep down the dark. Similarly, too much of eternal Project Management coaching can only polish the surface, and we leave the motivational speaker all whined with new ideas but found it sputter when we are back in the office.

I am sure many will curse me or scold me after reading this article, but let me clarify that I am the biggest fan of all external project resources, coaching, and certifications. Still, here the problem is, are this so-called partner in the process is willing to get to know you, your organization, your culture the way you do? If yes, they would have sticked you in front of the mirror and told you to have a word with yourself!

Having this in my mind and with the inspiration from Michael Jackson, I present the Project Man(ager) in the mirror. Now I will share what I did there, and from here, you are kind of on your own.

I blocked some time in my calendar, stood in front of a mirror, took a long hard look at myself, how I have managed my projects, and the people on whom my project success depends. Then I started asking some tough questions to myself about me! Those questions are the following.

- Are my methods being up to date?
- Do I cut corners?
- Am I listening to the team with proper attention?
- Do I sometimes settle for good, whereas I can strive for the best?
- Do I have the right people in the right place?
- Are there gaps in my thinking and the way I am doing things?
- Can I be benefited by doing multiple Project Manager certifications?
- Can I be benefited by attending multiple Project Management related webinars?
- Can I recommend my organization for complementary Project management services?

Honesty is the key to get the answer; the more honest you are, the more you could get out of these questions. The more that we drill down with these questions, the more uncomfortable it will get, and yes, sometimes it can be painful, but it's worth it, and it's worth more than spending your time, energy, and money on certifications, courses, textbooks, and webinars. This small and affordable exercise can gain you the worth of the millions, billions, and sometimes trillions because through this exercise, you will get the freedom to move forward more prominently and boldly. Simultaneously, it can pay you back big time and form the basis of very powerful personal and strengthen your roots as a great leader and team mission statement.

      Now that all of you would have a question in mind, that this exercise can also be done by a Project Management coach or maybe by a life coach more effectively. The answer is easy; no one knows you better than yourself; if you refer to a coach, make sure that the coach knows more about you than yourself! I know, and I am sure that is impossible, so do this exercise by yourself or with a partner you can trust. You can also be brutally honest with them; then I recommend you to do this exercise with them, and trust me, you will get out more than your expectation.Having said this, I did this exercise with myself some years back, and I have introduced a lot of positive changes to myself and my project management approach.

It may help you recognize some of these in yourself, but it may not also because it is ultimately as personal as one's fingerprint. So, here is what I came away with my-self mirror analysis.

Listen more than I talk.
Some years back, through this "Self-Mirror Analysis" exercise. I have realized that I am an "over-talkative" person. Being a Project Leader of various strategic projects, I had a habit of telling everyone how it would be. By harnessing this habit of mine, I found that my communication became focused, which means everyone better understood my version. The project team felt that they were being listened to and engaged with projects. Due to the change I bought within me by just doing the "Self-Mirror Analysis," the project team started coming up with ideas that are not bad.

I love the admin work:
I had a mindset that the admin side of Project Management work is just a sheer pain, a chore, and thus I had fallen into the trap of making mental notes. Through the "Self-Mirror Analysis," I realized the difference between good and great PMs. Initial days of my career, I am always impressed by PMs who can promptly answer a question, update the status of a Project, and share the right data as if these are part of their DNA. Till I did the "Self-Mirror Analysis," I was always thinking that writing notes and using PM software to store the information are a sheer waste of time.

However, after the analysis, my client started to see the difference easily; by the way, I started representing the data because I realized that answering the questions promptly, providing the status update, and sharing the right data is not in anyone's DNA. Still, we will have to inject that into our DNA. Thus, my client started to see the difference, and they started to banking on my Project data as critical data/ information.

It is a team game, and there is no concept of King and kinsmen.

From Planning to execution, from celebrating victories to laying blame, I established myself as an autonomous PM, treating my team as "Gofers." I had developed a culture of blame. Usually, when things went wrong, the gofer would be hauled, and "what went wrong" would be analyzed. It was all done with the best intention, but it was affecting the team's morale. After I did the "Self-Mirror Analysis," it changed drastically because I start giving importance to the team rather than thinking of myself as King and others as kinsmen. Things changed, and a collective responsibility emerged within the team, and suddenly everyone had everyone else's back.

Culture by design

The culture wasn't that great before, and it was one of the things that I always complain to my wife over dinner. I realized that I could design and deliver a great culture, but not sure where things are going wrong.

So, after I did the "Self-Mirror Analysis," I realized that the commoditization of IT means one can build a project piece by piece based on specific needs, so equally, a great culture is built bit by bit. As part of my analysis, I immediately replaced the long, dull meetings with quick catch-ups, interesting, engaging discussion, injected humor into the process, chats, emails wherever possible, and replaced the phone conversations with actual face-to-face wherever possible. Finally, it had become a natural environment ready to produce successful outcomes.

Conclusion

To conclude, these four points can allow a good project team to grow into a great one; I have made other improvements, but the key takeaway is that all such improvements came about through a little honest introspection. So each of you can try this, if you have a coach, colleague, and partner whom you can trust, then you can take their help to do this exercise, but I still recommend to try this out yourself, because at some point in your professional journey you have to be strong and continue your journey all alone. All the colleagues, coaches, mentors, and friends can help you only to a certain extent. All the aspiring project managers should give it a try to start with a whole new perspective. If you don't try this out, then remember the mirror still be there.

Disclaimer: Views expressed in this article are my own. I have articulated this article based on my experience of transforming myself from a stereotypical Project Manager to a free Spirit Project Manager. I hope this "Self-Mirror Analysis would work for all of you. Please do let me know how you found this analysis.

Disclaimer

This book is a structural representation of all my articles, which I published on multiple platforms like LinkedIn, PMToday, IAPM Blog, PMTimes, Medium.com, and Novel Vista. Most of the articles are based on my views and expression. Some of them, I have written based on my research. I have referred to some of the documents and artifacts in such cases—those links I have provided at the end of the chapter as reference. I have provided the reference link and disclaimer towards each chapter's end to clarify to all my readers.

About the Author

Abhishek Mishra aims to create a new platform or forum to facilitate discussion when people or leaders feel stuck and confused or unable to add value. He wanted to create a platform where people help and support each other, where there is no gender differentiation and where people become role models for each other.

As a writer, he has accomplished and accolades how he expressed his feelings through his words. He has written 50+ articles that were liked by many professionals over platforms like LinkedIn, medium.com, PM Today, PM Times and NovelVista

When he is not writing books, you can find him doing project management, and when he is not doing either of these, you can find him baking fabulous cakes.

Oh, man! It would be best if you tried his cakes and pastries. He is the kind of person who has loads of energy and does not like to sit idle.

His first book — "The Book of Powerful & Exceptional Quotes, was released on 26th May-2020. The book is a personal collection of quotes and quotes based on Abhishek's life experiences.

His Second book – "Stereotypical Leadership," was released on 9th July- 2020. The book has the power to transform a leader to be a great leader.

He has got stunning writing skills, Culinary skills, and strong management skills; not just that, he is also a process-oriented person. In a way, he always keeps trying different things, and this replicates his inquisitive nature too.

Professionally he is a project manager, so he has been associated with multiple non-profitable groups to learn and discover ways to help the community and society. You can connect with him at https://www.linkedin.com/in/abhishek-author/.

Apart from writing and project management, Abhishek provides services like ghost-writing, Resume writing, editing, proofreading, content review services on demand. His writing skills may be confirmed independently through his books.

For queries & questions related to the book and for any collaboration, please write to him at authorabhishek1206@gmail.com.

www.ingramcontent.com/pod-product-compliance
Lightning Source LLC
Chambersburg PA
CBHW031618210526
45464CB00004B/1629